WHERE DID WE GO WRONG

Charles A. Bell

ACKNOWLEDGEMENTS

I would like to thank…

God for giving me the inspiration, passion,
and opportunity to write this book

My grandmother, Deborah Burrell, for her words of
wisdom and praise. Throughout the rough times,
it was your words that helped me carry on

My mother, father, sister, uncles, aunts, and cousins for their
continued support over the years

DeAndre Stokes, Jason Hayes, Kevin Kemp and Jerome
Moulden for their commitment to community activism in
Detroit. Each of you will always be my brothers of the struggle

All of my friends from University Public Schools, Denby High
School, Wayne State University, Michigan State University, etc. Over
the years, I have become increasingly frustrated with the lack of
solutions to the problems in our community. It was my frustration
and our "intense" conversations that led me to write this book

Sabrina Cotton, for her generosity and support with this book.
Writing a book is a time consuming task, and I thank you for your
patience and input on these issues

TABLE OF CONTENTS

FOREWORD

Brothers and sisters, it is with great frustration that I write the pages enclosed within this book. Despite the progress we made during the Civil Rights Era, statistics still show a troublesome reality for African Americans in higher education, employment, homeownership, and political activism. As I write this book, I can only wonder how did a people who were filled with such pride and determination become so complacent with the subpar quality of housing, education, and government services we receive in the inner city? The compelling evidence enclosed within this book will show that we have a serious problem regarding the progress of black men and the overall black community. We have allowed a generation of black men to be overwhelmingly influenced by a culture that promotes the trafficking of drugs and death to our youth. Brothers and sisters, this is unacceptable! The purpose of this book is not to merely criticize and depict the flaws in our community but to ignite the moral vigor that we have since lost. Change is a choice—and today we must choose a different course because I fear what the future holds for us as a people. If you are brave enough to confront the problems that have plagued our progress in order to construct a better future for our people, join the struggle with me and turn the page. Change is indeed necessary and CHANGE begins TODAY...

Remembering Martin Luther King's Dream...

I once had a dream that I spoke to Martin Luther King
He said it seems like his people forgot about his dream
Martin said he had never seen such futile things
Black men murdering over blue, red, and green ($$)
With his head held down as he walked through my door
He asked, "Brother what did I put my life on the line for?"
Garvey, Dubois, Douglass...we all paved the way
Where are the leaders for our people today?

INTRODUCTION

As a Detroit, Michigan native and first generation college graduate, I am very familiar with the struggle associated with residing in an impoverished environment. The vast majority of my life has been shaped by a residence in which drugs, crime, and death were uncontrolled. I recall several homework assignments in elementary school that required us to write letters to the mayor, Dennis Archer, requesting an increased police presence in our community. I remember vividly the almost daily drive-by shootings and being asked to sell crack cocaine at the age of twelve years old. Although those experiences appeared to be appalling in the least, it was those events that motivated me to pursue my education and question the world around me.

Did your high school education prepare you for college or to secure employment? Why does Wayne State University graduate less than 15 percent of its black students in six years? Why do Detroit Public Schools graduate less than sixty-five percent of their students in four years? Where was I supposed to learn about credit? Did I miss that course in high school? Where was I supposed to learn proper interview skills? Who was supposed to teach me how to find a job? Where was I supposed to learn how to purchase a home? What is a Fico score? What are interest rates? Who determines how interest rates vary? What are stocks? What are bonds? Did I miss the course where we discussed the benefits and drawbacks of a 401k?

As the world began to unfold before my eyes, I recognized that despite my above average academic performance, my preparation for the "real world" was noticeably deficient in many areas. It didn't take long for me to realize that information regarding credit, investing, homeownership, job seeking skills, African American history, and the essentials for success in the global economy were absent from our classrooms. Still, none of the previous questions is more disheartening than the ones I have yet to propose. Why is this information absent from our school curriculum? Shouldn't it be there?

The purpose of this book is to explore research from the Civil Rights Era to present day, in order to show a multitude of serious problems that have hindered the progress made by African Americans in educational attainment, homeownership, political activism, and in the judicial system. It is my belief that numerous factors on a systematic and cultural level have contributed to the problems that have manifested in the African American community. Once we engage in solution-oriented discourse, collectively we can solve these problems and change the future for our people.

EDUCATION

We have a PROBLEM in EDUCATION!

In regards to education we have a serious problem in the African American community. We know we have a problem, we have heard repeatedly that there is a problem, but we have not heard how bad the problem is. If you are wondering how grim the outlook is for African American men, you will not need to look any further. A report titled "The Ominous Gender Gap in African American Higher Education" stated "If we project into the future the losses black men have consistently logged over the past twenty years, by the year 2097, women will earn **ALL** of the bachelor's degrees awarded to blacks in the United States (6)."[1] The figures on the next page use data provided by the U.S. Department of Education to show the significant increase in associate and bachelor's degrees conferred to African American females, while their male counterparts lag behind. Collectively, African American women earned 103,142 bachelor's degrees in 2009, while African American men earned 53,473 bachelor's degrees.[2] In the same year African American women also earned 69,493 associate's degrees while African American men earned only 17,829 associate's degrees.

African American Bachelor Degree Attainment

	Men	Women
1976		
2009		

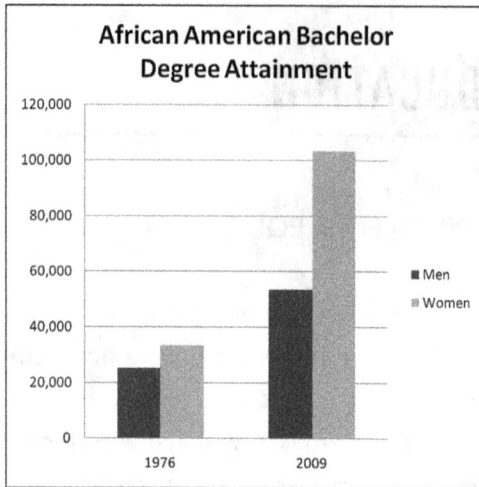

Source: U.S. Department of Education, National Center for Education Statistics, Higher Education General Information Survey (HEGIS), "Degrees and Other Formal Awards Conferred" surveys, 1976-77 and 1980-81; and 1989-90 through 2008-09 Integrated Postsecondary Education Data System, "Completions Survey" (IPEDS-C:90-99), and Fall 2000 through Fall 2009.

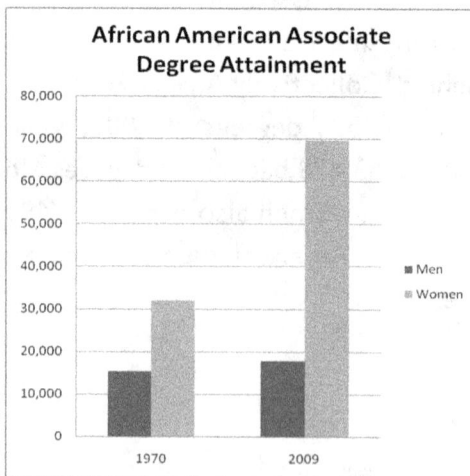

African American Associate Degree Attainment

How do we explain the drastic increase in African American female graduation rates? Are parents encouraging black females to pursue academics while simultaneously discouraging black males from pursing similar opportunities? Are our schools failing to address the needs and/or interests of African American males? What is going on in our schools? When comparing the number of African American male and female degree recipients in 2009, I cannot help but wonder, "Where are African American men if they are not in our classrooms?"

2

Although research often places a great emphasis on college graduation rates, in order to explore the issue of African American male educational attainment we must first identify the barriers that exist in K-12 education. In 2010 the Schott 50 State Report on Public Education and Black Males reported the national high school cohort graduation rate for African American men was 47% in the 2007-2008 academic year.[3] Furthermore, states such as Nevada and Florida graduate less than one-third of their African American male students within the designated four-year period.[4] One question that immediately comes to mind is at what point in our education system do black men fall through the cracks? Well, brothers and sisters education researchers have known for decades that African American boys are over-represented in special education and school discipline settings. Still, the lack of progress researchers and practitioners have made in reducing African American representation in those settings is appalling. A study performed by Dr. Llyod Dunn, a former professor of special education at the University of Hawaii, in 1968 found that African Americans collectively represented <u>fifteen percent of the school-age population</u> and <u>thirty-eight percent of those in special education</u>.[4] Over twenty years later, a different study found that those numbers changed to <u>sixteen percent and thirty-five percent respectively</u>.[5] Since additional research shows there is a 4:1 ratio of African American males to African American females in special education, it is evident that our special education system is problematic.[6]

Although the statistics above may be shocking, the purpose of this exploration is to initiate solution-oriented discourse. Now that we are aware a problem exists, we must be critical of our education system. At this point you may be asking yourself why do African American boys make up such a significant percentage of special education enrollments nationwide? Is the fact that nearly ninety percent of K-12 teachers and practicing school psychologists are Caucasian contributing to a higher referral rate for African American students due to a lack of understanding of our culture?[7,8] Dr. Laurie Ford, school psychology professor at the University of Kansas, and her colleagues stated "Given the possibility of over identification of African American students for special education services, it is important that all school professionals, particularly school psychologists, deliver culturally sensitive services (298)."[9] Are school personnel providing culturally sensitive services in our schools? Is there some sort of racial bias embedded in the special education referral process? Are IQ tests biased against black students? Are African American parents de-emphasizing the importance of education and steering our youth toward careers in entertainment and sports? It is important for us to acknowledge that all of these factors could be contributing to the disproportionate representation of African American boys in special education and we need to do something about it *immediately*.

In order to identify the root of the problem, we must investigate the practices of special education programs. Dr. Donald Oswald and Dr. Matha Coutinho, professors of psychiatry and special education respectively, investigated African American over-representation in the mild mental retardation (MMR) and serious emotional disability (SED) categories by utilizing survey data from nearly 43,000 schools across the nation.[10] Drs. Oswald and Coutinho concluded that nationally African American students were two and one-half times more likely to receive a diagnosis of mild mental retardation and one and one-half times more likely to receive a serious emotional disability diagnosis when compared to non-African American students. The researchers also concluded that environmental variables such as household income and parents' highest educational attainment influenced the likelihood of receiving an MMR diagnosis. Despite the researcher's explanation, you may be asking yourself questions such as who determines if a student is mentally retarded? What type of tasks must a student show deficiency in to receive a label of "mild mental retardation"? Since less than thirty percent of students who are placed in special education graduate high school, why do school personnel continue to place such degrading and long-lasting labels on children?[35] Instead of asking what is wrong with black children, should we be asking what is wrong with our education system?

The Detroit Free Press[11]

"Special-education students in Michigan lost 251,410 hours of instruction during the 2010-2011 school year because they were suspended or expelled from school.

And 20 school districts have been identified as having a disproportionate number of black special-education students who are kicked out of school.

The numbers concern Eleanor White, director of the Office of Special Education at the Michigan Department of Education. Michigan schools educated more than 200,000 special-education students during that school year. And White said if the neediest kids aren't in school, they're not learning. That makes them more likely to be retained or to drop out (Detroit Free Press, 2012)."

The New York Times[12]

"Most students who are enrolled in special education classes in New York City are failing to earn regular high school diplomas, according to a study released yesterday by a nonprofit group that monitors the school system.

About 111,000 students who received special education services left the system from 1996 to 2004, and of those students,

13,672 - or 12.3 percent - graduated with Regents or local diplomas, according to Advocates for Children, the nonprofit group that issued the report, "Leaving Empty-Handed." In addition, 12 percent received an alternative certificate, an Individualized Education Program diploma.

"The graduation rates are grim and mean that most of the city's students receiving special education services are leaving school with no options for college, employment or independence," said Jill Chaifetz, the executive director of the group (New York Times, 2005)."

The figure on the right features statistics from the San Francisco Unified School District (SFUSD). While African Americans comprise 10.8% of the students enrolled in the San Francisco school district, they represent 22.8% of those in enrolled in special education, 28.1% of students who were diagnosed with a specific learning disability, and 47% of those who are classified as "Emotionally disturbed."

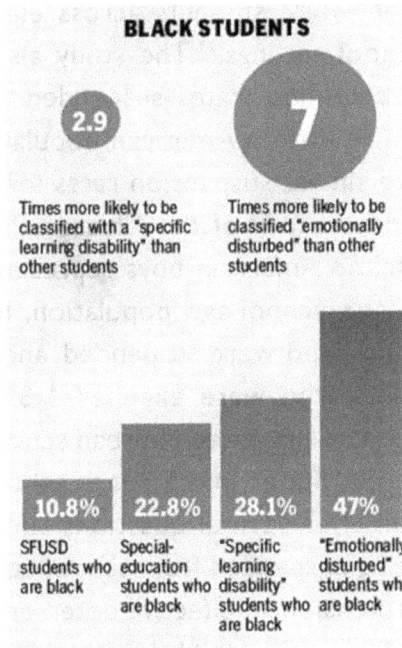

BLACK STUDENTS

2.9

Times more likely to be classified with a "specific learning disability" than other students

7

Times more likely to be classified "emotionally disturbed" than other students

| 10.8% | 22.8% | 28.1% | 47% |

| SFUSD students who are black | Special-education students who are black | "Specific learning disability" students who are black | "Emotionally disturbed" students who are black |

Source: The University of California Berkeley

Typically, when you think of California you think of Hollywood, million-dollar mansions, and an abundance of wealth. Yet, research has shown that problems pertaining to African American educational attainment stem far beyond impoverished areas and into some of the wealthiest school districts in our country.

Although African American special education referral rates are a very serious issue, this is not the only significant issue that influences educational outcomes in K-12 settings. The disproportionate representation of African American males in school discipline settings (i.e. suspension, expulsion, etc) is an equally important issue that requires major attention. In 1975, the Children's Defense Fund analyzed national school suspension data and concluded that black students were suspended nearly three times more often than white students across elementary, middle, and high school settings.[13] The study also showed that more than twenty-nine states suspended over five percent of their entire African American population while only four states had similar suspension rates for white students. In 2009, a federal study of the Chicago Public School system found African American boys represented twenty-three percent of the school-age population, forty-four percent of students who were suspended, and sixty-one percent of students who were expelled.[14] Sadly, similar statistics have been documented in urban school districts throughout the United States. In regards to school suspension, we must ask ourselves several questions such as why are our children being suspended from school at such a high rate? Is school suspension an effective deterrent or does it promote poor behavior? If a child does not want to attend school, he or she can simply perform an act that would warrant suspension. By incorporating such a practice in our public schools, are we disconnecting our students from the classroom and consequently sending them to the streets?

The school suspension issue is of particular interest to me because I have been suspended several times due to poor behavior. As a student who excelled academically but struggled behaviorally, I can honestly say that being suspended was a poor punishment because it only made me more popular with the wrong crowd. The idea that schools could actually be contributing to the "school to prison pipeline" by disconnecting students from their academic environment is rarely acknowledged, because it would force school personnel to use alternative methods for dealing with problematic students. However, we must ask ourselves if this is a bad thing? Should we **be pushing our students out of school** in order to encourage **them to pay attention and perform well in school?** IT DOES NOT MAKE SENSE! At this point you may be asking yourself if educators and policy makers are aware that school suspension is not a good solution for most problematic students, why is this tactic used so freely in our schools? Don't worry I am wondering that too...

Early education research highlights several factors that may play a role in the disproportionate representation of African American males in school discipline settings. Still, one of the more legitimate theories during this time was that "poverty" may play a large role in explaining the higher suspension rates seen in African American populations. Dr. Shi-Chang Wu, an education researcher at John Hopkins University, and several of his colleagues conducted one of the initial studies that investigated school suspension data to determine if a relationship existed between socioeconomic status (i.e. household income) and suspension rates.[15] Using data collected by the Safe School Study, Dr. Wu and his colleagues analyzed survey data from more than 4500 schools at the elementary, middle, and high school levels. Dr. Wu's study found that students whose fathers were not employed full-time exhibited higher suspension rates than students whose fathers had full-time employment. In addition, Wu and his colleagues concluded that students who received free lunch were suspended at higher rates than students who did not receive such subsidies. Although on the surface it appears that fathers and school lunches are directly related to suspension rates, a more realistic explanation of Dr. Wu's conclusions could be that students who receive free lunch subsidy typically reside in lower income households and in neighborhoods where violent behavior is prevalent. Also, many of the children who stated their father was not employed full-time may not have a father who was actively involved in their life. All of these factors increase the likelihood that a child will exhibit poor behavior in academic settings.

Despite the fact that a residence in an impoverished environment may contribute to a student's poor academic performance, research and personal experience prove that the environment does not "always" mean he or she will perform poorly. Research shows in early childhood the parent-child relationship significantly impacts the child's selection of friends and the quality of future relationships.[16] Understanding the importance of the parent-child relationship and how this bond influences future relationships shows us how positive parenting can help a child achieve desired academic outcomes. Parental supervision and the use of consistent and reasonable discipline is proven to decrease the risk of problematic behavior in children. Thus, parents have an extremely important role in providing adequate supervision, support, and discipline in order to teach their children how to conduct themselves at home and in their classroom.

Since research has informed us that parents and socioeconomic status may play a role in the disproportionate suspension of African American boys, you may be asking yourself if school personnel also contribute to this problem. Yes, they most certainly do! In 1999 Dr. Russel Skiba, professor in counseling and educational psychology at Indiana University, analyzed data from disciplinary records of 11,001 students across 19 middle schools and found that African American students were suspended at higher rates regardless of socioeconomic status.[17] In the past, researchers thought "poverty" alone may be able to explain high suspension rates, but what causes African Americans to be suspended so frequently when they reside in middle class households? What causes African Americans to be suspended at such high rates when crime is not prevalent in their environment? Dr. Skiba found that African Americans were suspended more frequently for **nonviolent** and subjective offenses such **as disrespect, excessive noise, and loitering than white students.**[18] The results of this study are so shocking that we must ask ourselves are school personnel intimidated by black students? Are our children being suspended disproportionately because it is easier for the school to exclude them than to reach them in the classroom?

In 2004 Dr. Ann Gregory, psychology professor at Rutgers University, and Pharmicia Mosely, graduate student at the University of California Berkeley, conducted a study that investigated school personnel's perceptions of causal factors related to school discipline.[18] Using semi-structured interviews, they found fifty percent of the teachers' responses fell in the "teacher's belief" category, which states teachers perceive African American students as dangerous individuals therefore they refer them for discipline at higher rates than students of other racial backgrounds. Although this study only featured 19 teachers from one particular school, the results definitely make you wonder how many teachers in your school share similar beliefs regarding African American students. Is your child a target simply because he or she is black?

Before we place complete blame on the school system, school personnel, or environmental factors we must first realize that this is our problem. Nobody else is going to come save the day! We have to work together in order to help our people! School suspension is a serious issue because if your child is not in school, he or she is not being educated and the risk for juvenile delinquency is significantly increased. We must take an aggressive stance against anything that interferes with education, because we have lost so many of our children to prison and death. Research shows that when considering the variables that influence juvenile delinquency, the **quality of parenting a child** receives may be a greater influence than risk factors for negative outcomes such as low socioeconomic status and early exposure to violence. The fact that the quality of parenting a child receives has a greater impact on educational outcomes than environmental risk factors proves that we control our own destiny.

In addition to the quality of parenting a child receives, parental involvement in education is critical to a child's success. Why do African American parents have such low turnouts at parent-teacher's conferences? How can we expect our children to have a chance at a good career, if we do not support them? In my experience, many parents who were not successful in school feel intimidated by the academic environment and do not understand how their presence could help their child. I would like all of my readers to understand that regardless of your education, income, or marital status your support in our schools is invaluable. WE NEED YOU! Also, I encourage teachers to make the academic environment more welcoming for parents. It is unrealistic to expect parents to magically walk in the door and participate without some cooperation on your behalf. I remember during my academic years, my teachers and parents played a significant role in my success, because they saw my potential and challenged me to be a better student. Such support and motivation were critical for me at times because my poor behavior overshadowed my academic success. However, with support, from my parents and teachers, I was able to defy the odds and obtain a masters degree from Michigan State University by the age of 24. With your support, your child can accomplish this and so much more!

The diagram on the left shows the percentage of students who passed the Michigan Merit Exam in the Bloomfield Hills School District.

Percentage of students who passed MME, split by the three largest demographics

	Students	Reading	Writing	Math	Science	Social Studies
2011	District-IA	83%	76%	76%	78%	87%
	White	87%	82%	80%	82%	89%
	Black	53%	37%	40%	45%	70%
	Asian	94%	87%	100%	97%	100%

(Black students average 35% lower than white students, 47% lower than Asian students)

	Students	Reading	Writing	Math	Science	Social Studies
2010	District-IA	86%	74%	78%	81%	94%
	White	89%	80%	82%	85%	97%
	Black	69%	43%	49%	54%	83%
	Asian	91%	84%	91%	84%	91%

(Black students average 27% lower than white students, 29% lower than Asian students)

	Students	Reading	Writing	Math	Science	Social Studies
2009	District-IA	83%	77%	73%	79%	91%
	White	87%	83%	78%	83%	93%
	Black	54%	25%	29%	44%	78%
	Asian	81%	79%	90%	93%	93%

(Black students average 40% lower than white students, 41% lower than Asian students)

Source: www.michigan.gov/mme

Bloomfield Hills is a metro Detroit suburb that typically comprises families from middle and upper class backgrounds and features low violent crime. In 2009, only 25% of African Americans in the Bloomfield Hills School District passed the writing portion of the Michigan Merit exam, while 83% of white students and 79% of Asian students were able to achieve passing scores. Although in 2011 African Americans showed some improvement, they clearly lag behind white and Asian students. How can we explain such poor test scores in a school district that is not impoverished? Why do our students consistently lag behind? Please look carefully at this figure and ask yourself WHY?

After taking a serious look at the figure above we must realize the problems in our education system stem far beyond money. In my opinion the achievement gap between black and non-black students in Metro Detroit and in many urban areas is the result of systemic problems on both a cultural and school personnel level. On the cultural level, many African Americans in urban areas like Detroit have pursued careers that did not require substantial academic work (i.e. manufacturing); therefore, we have multiple generations that do not know how to guide their children through school. The fact that our parents and grandparents were likely educated in the same dysfunctional school systems increases our disadvantage. The challenging times of today reveal, now more than ever, young metro Detroiters cannot rely on jobs in the automotive field as their parents and grandparents were able to. Problems pertaining to school personnel are deeply rooted in the preparation they receive for work in urban settings. As a graduate of one of these programs, I know that school personnel are often trained under the false notion that an abundance of resources will be available to them in the "real world". Once the school personnel member realizes that his/her job is more difficult without the use of such resources, he or she is likely to contribute to the dysfunctional practices already in motion within the institution. The figure on the next page provides a concept map of this phenomenon.

The Achievement Gap between Black and White Students: Bell's Concept Map

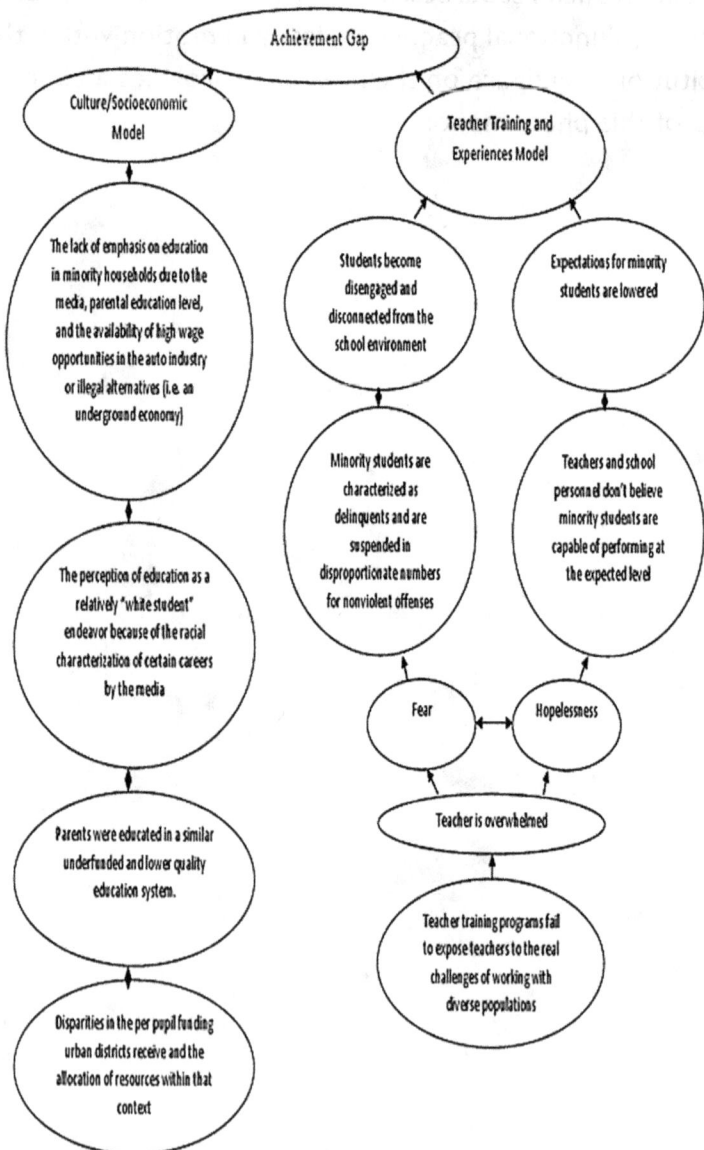

Achievement Gap

Culture/Socioeconomic Model

Teacher Training and Experiences Model

The lack of emphasis on education in minority households due to the media, parental education level, and the availability of high wage opportunities in the auto industry or illegal alternatives (i.e. an underground economy)

Students become disengaged and disconnected from the school environment

Expectations for minority students are lowered

Minority students are characterized as delinquents and are suspended in disproportionate numbers for nonviolent offenses

Teachers and school personnel don't believe minority students are capable of performing at the expected level

The perception of education as a relatively "white student" endeavor because of the racial characterization of certain careers by the media

Fear

Hopelessness

Parents were educated in a similar underfunded and lower quality education system.

Teacher is overwhelmed

Teacher training programs fail to expose teachers to the real challenges of working with diverse populations

Disparities in the per pupil funding urban districts receive and the allocation of resources within that context

My Vision for Urban Education

I have thought long and hard about solutions to the problems that have manifested in urban school districts. My vision for urban education involves addressing these problems in three areas: 1) Policy, 2) Within School, and 3) Community.

Tier I – Policy

As teachers, administrators, school personnel members, and/or students from urban environments, we are all aware that many of the problems that plague urban education need to be addressed at a policy level. A substantial amount of the funding public schools receive comes from property tax revenue. Therefore, when you compare cities that have drastically different home values, such as Bronx, New York and Manhasset, New York, a disparity in funding is unavoidable. **There is no excuse for the continuation of a school funding system that knowingly perpetuates inequality.**

The New York Daily News[19]

"New York State ranks near the bottom of the country in how fairly it funds its schools, asserts a new Rutgers University report released Tuesday.

Only four other states have a bigger gap between how much money they send to their poorest schools compared with their wealthiest ones, researchers at Rutgers and the Education Law Center in New Jersey found.

"It really gives us pause," said Geri Palast, head of the Campaign for Fiscal Equity, the group that filed a successful lawsuit in the 1990s to force the state to fund poor schools more equitably.

New York spends more on education overall than most other states, but researchers call its funding methods "regressive."

Wealthy districts rely on high property taxes to fund their schools - a luxury many poor districts do not have.

As a result, in 2008, a New York school district with no poor kids received about $17,000 per student in local and state aid, while one with at least 30% of the students living in poverty got about $14,000 per student (New York Daily News, 2010)."

When policy makers decided to fund schools using property taxes, the best minds of our time came together to propose this method. We need the most creative and innovative thinkers to come back to the table and help structure our education system to address the needs of our time and the future. Issues such as the lack of cross cultural training many school personnel members receive, incentives for teacher performance, and improved standards of proficiency need to be addressed.

Tier II – Within Schools

Within each individual school system lies a structured and unique culture that can be regulated by its leaders.

For example, research has shown that schools that have administrators who advocate alternative methods for solving students' behavior problems tend to have a much lower suspension rate than schools with administrators who adopt zero tolerance policies.[20] I highlight this example because school suspension in urban settings is "out of control" and it places the educators in a position where they are indirectly contributing to the achievement gap. Teachers suspend students everyday for "fighting" and conducting other unacceptable behaviors without directly teaching them what's appropriate. We can argue that parents are supposed to teach their children acceptable conflict resolution techniques, but the fact is that **it's not being taught and somebody needs to step up and fill that void.** I believe the education a population receives should be a reflection of the needs of that population. If these children have unique behavioral needs, we should address them.

In addition to regulating the school culture, we also need to adapt the curriculum to the students. In my opinion, our education system is very rigid, closed minded, and it forces the student to either adapt or seek alternative endeavors. In the 21st century, education needs to be a bi-directional process where the system adapts to the interests and learning styles of the students while also allowing the students to provide input on the curriculum. A textbook should not be the absolute beginning and end of all learning. Our children need job preparation, a concrete understanding of technology, and the skills necessary to **exceed expectations**. How difficult would it be to incorporate homeownership lessons or investing strategies into a math course? if we take our children's lives seriously, they will take school and their own lives seriously.

Tier III – Community

During the span from 1970 -1980's African American academic achievement increased substantially. It appears the increase in educational attainment was the product of direct involvement in the community and the promotion of positive outcomes. Support from parents was high because the parents associated directly with teachers and administrators. In many urban schools today, parent-teacher conferences typically yield low turnouts and schools take few measures to regain parental support. Parents cannot be purchased through "pizza parties" or "ice cream socials." Dedicated administrators must employ innovative methods to convey the urgency of this situation and the need for support. The low graduation rates and high incarceration rates cannot be "sugar coated" because this is the reality of the situation in urban school districts.

The purpose of presenting this information is so we can all agree that educational attainment in the African American community is not solely an issue of money, availability of resources, or personnel. It is not solely the teachers' or school psychologists' fault that our children are not successful in school. We must ask ourselves why do we accept a system in which our children are not successful? Why do public schools have such poor parent involvement when our children are at such a high risk for academic failure? **DO WE CARE?** We have allowed our education system to have complete control over our children's future and it is time for us to take that control back! Brothers and sisters....we can do better! I am tired of seeing my people uneducated, poor, and ill prepared for the demands of our society. Earlier in this chapter I asked if black men are not enrolled and/or graduating from higher education programs where are they? Please turn the page and view the two figures. Sadly, this is where a large portion of our brothers are and will remain until we address their needs in the classroom and in our community.

INCARCERATION

Incarceration: *The School to Prison Pipeline*

United States Population
by Race Census Year 2000

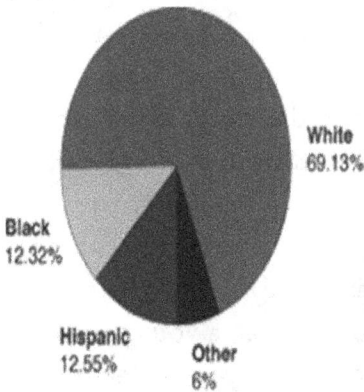

United States Prison
Population by Race Census Year
2000

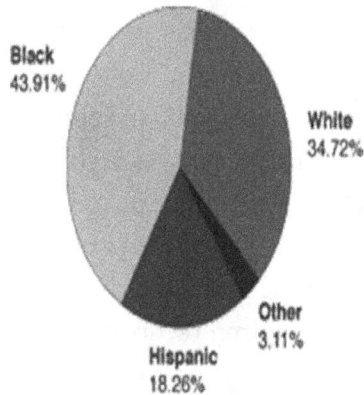

White
69.13%

Black
12.32%

Hispanic
12.55%

Other
6%

Black
43.91%

White
34.72%

Hispanic
18.26%

Other
3.11%

Source: "Incarcerated America: Human Rights Watch Backgrounder." Human Rights Watch (2003), http://www.hrw.org/legacy/backgrounder/usa/incarceration/us042903.pdf

One of the biggest problems with the wide use of school suspension is that we disconnect students from the school setting and indirectly contribute to the school to prison pipeline. Although we don't intentionally cause students to form gangs or perform deviant acts, we must be aware of the potential consequences of suspending students in such high numbers. Dr. Marc Mauer, assistant director of The Sentencing Project, stated one-third of black men between the ages of twenty and twenty-nine were either incarcerated, on probation, or on parole.[21] We must ask ourselves what is the difference between the one-third of black men in this age group who are in some phase of the correction system and the two-thirds of black men who managed to avoid this outcome? In terms of past experiences or behaviors, the most notable difference between these two groups is high school dropout.[22] Specifically, individuals who drop out of school at the age of sixteen were four times more likely to be incarcerated at ages nineteen to twenty-two.[22] If researchers and policy makers know that high school drop out at the age of sixteen is associated with higher incarceration rates, **why is it legal for students to drop out at this age?** Why don't our schools dedicate more resources to raising awareness of the association between high school dropout and incarceration rates? Lastly, why do we allow our children to drop out of school at such a young age if we are aware of the potential consequences of this decision? It may be difficult to convince a 16 year old to stay in school but if we start at a young age we can set a better foundation for our children and significantly improve incarceration rates. WE CAN DO BETTER!

Between the years 2000 and 2007 the incarceration rate for African American men was 6.5 times that of Caucasian men and 2.5 times that of Hispanic men.[22] Why are African American men imprisoned at such high rates? Has the influx of rappers and entertainers that embrace criminal lifestyles translated into a greater acceptance of incarceration in our community?

Number of arrests, by type of drug law violations, 1982-2007

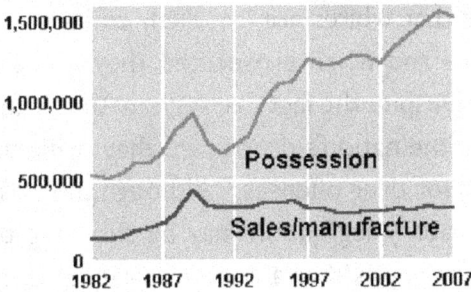

1,500,000					
1,000,000					
500,000	Possession				
	Sales/manufacture				
0					
1982	1987	1992	1997	2002	2007

Do lawmakers disproportionately target men of color in our society? Why don't we actively discourage crime in our community? Do phrases such as, "Get it how you live", "I'm a product of my environment", or "Snitches Get Stitches" indicate a general acceptance of a criminal lifestyle in our community? There use to be a time where you could not sell drugs in the black community because activists discouraged such behavior. How did we deviate from those times to where we are today?

The drastic increase in African American incarceration rates can be traced back to the influx of crack cocaine and heroin during the 1980s. Instead of directly limiting the availability of these illegal substances, our legislators passed the Anti-Drug Abuse Acts of 1986 and 1988 which created harsher sentences for drugs typically found in poor African American and Hispanic neighborhoods. Under the Anti-Drug Abuse Acts **selling five grams of crack cocaine** warranted a minimum five-year federal prison sentence, **while selling FIVE HUNDRED grams of powder cocaine warranted the same** sentence.[23, 24] Why does our government specifically target drugs distributed in poor African American and Hispanic neighborhoods? Shouldn't our government provide EQUAL punishment for the trafficking of ALL hardcore illegal substances? Do distributors of drugs typically found in white neighborhoods such as "crystal meth" just get a pass? After more than 20 years of implementing the Anti Drug Abuse acts, researchers have found that whites are less likely to be prosecuted for drug offenses and when prosecuted, they are less likely to be convicted.[25] Despite the fact that African Americans comprise nearly 15% of the nation's drug users, they make up 74% of those sentenced for drug offenses.[25] Although the existence of such discriminatory legislation may be shocking to some, what is more shocking is that a huge disparity in drug sentencing still exists today.

In light of the increase in the incarceration rates for African American men, one factor that is frequently ignored is how the absence of black men impacts black families. Research shows that once convicted for drug related offenses, black men are serving longer sentences than their white counterparts. The average sentence for crack cocaine possession and/or distribution for African Americans in 2003 was 123 months, which is 42 months longer than the sentence for powder cocaine offenses.[25] That means a mother, father, wife and/or child is robbed of the opportunity to spend quality time with that individual because our government embraces a disparity in drug sentencing. How is this fair? What message are we sending to our children by allowing such a disparity to exist? Research also shows the incarceration rate for African American women for all crimes has increased by **800%** since 1986, compared to 400% for women of other ethnicities predominately due to drug convictions.[26] With incarceration rates at such high levels in the African American community, studies estimate that one out of every fourteen African American children has a parent currently in prison. That means on average at least two children in your son or daughter's class have a parent who is in prison. A parent's job is to provide the foundation and guidance necessary to help a child successfully navigate trials and tribulations in this world. Brothers and sisters, we cannot raise our children from prison walls and collect phone calls! We have to do better...

Although the impact of incarceration is devastating to a family while he or she is imprisoned, it should be acknowledged that substantial improvement is not guaranteed upon the family member's release. As a result of spending time in prison, many individuals may lose the employment skills they acquired prior to incarceration. Also, a large number of prisoners have such low levels of education that they are not qualified for many positions. Dr. Joan Petersilia, professor in criminology at Stanford Law School, states nearly 40 percent of prisoners at the state and federal levels do not have a high school diploma or GED and a one-third have a physical or mental impairment that prevents them from working.[26] It is very clear that prison has a costly impact on the individual, family, and larger community. How do we encourage our brothers and sisters to consider alternatives that will not lead to this tragic outcome? Where are the black leaders who are suppose to actively denounce drug trafficking and promote education in our community? Are they lost? Did they miss the south side of Chicago? Did they forget about Detroit and Baltimore? Are they living the American Dream or Martin Luther King's Dream? Where are they?

In the midst of the education and incarceration crisis we have in our community, I have always wondered where are our leaders? It is clear that we have an elite group of leaders in our community and these individuals always appear on a national stage to denounce black-white crime or police brutality. Yet, we NEVER see these individuals in our community and they NEVER discuss black on black crime or issues that directly pertain to us. **Do police kill black men in record numbers, or do black men kill each other in record numbers?** We have a serious problem here...Al Sharpton...Jesse Jackson! We need leadership and we have never seen you in our community! I would love to see Al Sharpton in my neighborhood talking to the people he claims to represent on a national level. I would love to see Mr. Sharpton and Mr. Jackson come to my city and immerse themselves in the struggle my people endure every day. **I know you walked with Dr. King, Mr. Jackson, but we need you to walk with "us"! We need help! Where are you?**

It is clear that we need leadership in the African American community and that our current "leadership" is inept. They have failed to adapt to the problems we encounter in our community. Consequently, the real question we must ask ourselves is how do we start again? As we analyze the Civil Rights Movement, we can conclude that black leaders during this time directly addressed any and every issue that resulted in a negative outcome for our community. As Lea E. Williams stated in her book "Servants of the People: The 1960s Legacy of African American Leadership," "African American leaders of a bygone era struggled over vastly different issues. Their fight, also against insuperable odds, was to gain civil rights, equality, and dignity for blacks in a racially divided society that was pervasively separate and unequal. Whatever the tensions between moderates and militants, between those firmly vested in the capitalist system and those clearly working on the fringes — for the most part — those leaders were **servants of the people** who had a genuine desire to lift up the black community by eliminating the formidable obstacles to educational, social, economic, and political equality that existed. They left an undeniably dynamic legacy on which to build."[25] Brothers and sisters, we must not allow the efforts of Dr. King, Rosa Parks, W.E.B Dubois and several others to be in vain. The time for change has come! We must answer the calls of our people and **we must serve our people.**

In the 1980s hip hop music featured positive messages that inspired many African Americans to pursue college degrees and refrain from engaging in drug use or other criminal activity. Rap artists such as Slick Rick provided positive and thought-provoking messages in their lyrics such as

Slick Rick "Hey Young World"

This rap here... it may cause concern
Its Broad and deep... why don't you listen and learn
Love mean happiness... that once was strong
But due to society... even that's turned wrong
Times have changed... and its cool to look bummy
And be a dumb dummy and disrespect your mummy
Have you forgotten... who put you on this earth?
Who brought you up right... and who loved you since your birth?
Reward is a brainwashed kid goin wild
Young little girls already have a child
Bad company... hey, now you've been framed
Your parents are hurting... hurting and ashamed
You're ruining yourself... and your mommy cant cope
Hey, little kids don't follow these dopes

Nonetheless, over the years we have heard rap artists convey to children that selling drugs is cool and going to prison makes you popular. The image of a "thug" is deeply rooted in urban African American culture and main-stream music as evidenced by song lyrics such as Young Jeezy's "I Still Love It" where he references himself selling drugs and *frying in hell*, or Gucci Mane's "All White Bricks" where he states **if you want a "bad bitch" you have to sell "bricks"** (i.e. cocaine). In the song "Da Dopeman" rapper T.I. **describes the respect and glory an individual receives from selling crack cocaine.** When asked, "Where did we go wrong," a simple and obvious response is right here!

As a community, we have to be more aware of the messages embedded in music, movies, and other media outlets. Do you know what messages are embedded in the music your child, niece, or cousin listens to? Do you approve of the messages embedded in the songs above? As a child, I remember loudly reciting the chorus of Tupac's song "Ratha Be Ya Nigga" in my sister's room as the tape played in the cassette player. At the time, I had no idea what I was saying, but after reciting the chorus, which references drinking and smoking weed, my father angrily ran into the room and smashed the cassette on the floor. Although my father never explained to me why he broke the tape or the meaning of the words in Tupac's song, now I understand how devastating such messages can be to children. Also, when I reflect on my behavioral difficulties, I can see a direct correlation between the music I listened to and my school suspension record. At the age of 14, I purchased DMX's CD "It's Dark and Hell Is Hot" and the songs on this CD send a terrible message to our youth. I recall songs where DMX is talking to and performing murders on the behalf of Satan, whom DMX refers to as Damien. Also, the lyrics of DMX's song **"X is coming for you"** depict a very dark and grotesque scene of him **breaking into someone's home and forcing the parents of a girl to watch him rape their daughter.** Perhaps more shocking is the fact that DMX's CD achieved four times platinum status, or four million record sales, as of December 2000.[26]

Brothers and sisters how can we expect our children to become doctors, lawyers, accountants, etc if they are listening to music that conveys such negativity? Why are we surprised when our black men pursue the lifestyle of a drug dealer when we allow songs such as "Da Dopeman" to be played in our homes? Realistically, I know a parent cannot control every element of what their child listens to or is influenced by outside of their household but we need to have a serious discussion about these messages with our children. Our sons should not be proud of the degradation of females depicted in rap videos nor should our daughters pressure themselves to wear more revealing clothing in order to attract attention from boys. We have to raise our sons and daughters to become proud BLACK MEN and WOMEN. The future of our people depends on the decisions you make with your child.

It is a well-known fact that rap music videos portray negative stereotypical images of African American women. Supporting evidence shows that on average, adolescents watch nearly 3 ½ hours of music videos per day that depict females in a sexually explicit manner.[27,28] Dr. Gina Wingood, a professor in public health at Emory University, and her colleagues conducted a study that investigated the relationship between exposure to rap music videos and health-related outcomes for African American females. Dr. Wingood's study found that females who reported greater exposure to rap videos also reported a higher number of sexual partners, were more likely to test positive for sexually transmitted diseases, and engage in drug use.[29] Are these the outcomes we want for our black women? If we want the best for our black women we must DEMAND THE BEST! We must hold these entertainers accountable for the destructive images and messages they send to our youth. As a black man from Detroit, Michigan I am aware of the negativity we see in our neighborhoods and that rappers are entitled to discuss their experiences. However, if every multi-millionaire entertainer re-invested themselves in the community in a positive manner, we may not have these problems. Instead of money, cars, clothes, and "hoes", we could be in the community talking about homeownership, investing, and how to avoid the negative outcomes depicted in rap music. As a black entertainer, how can you make thirteen songs about selling drugs in the community and not take ownership of the damage you are doing?

Problems in the Black Community

1. The unemployment rate for African Americans is a critical issue that needs attention. Where are our leaders? Why are they not working in our communities to help us develop job-related skills? Why don't our schools teach students how to develop resumes or effectively utilize interview strategies? Are those skills not as valuable as learning English, math, and science?

2. African American adolescents are dropping out of school and engaging in criminal activity at very young ages. Given the near life-long consequences of not having a quality education and being incarcerated, we need to speak sincerely to our youth about the choices they make. We can do more to help our youth.

3. The poverty rate among African American families is a serious issue. We need to invest more of our money into our own businesses. Detroit, Michigan has the highest concentration of African Americans in the country. How many grocery stores, gas stations, or other businesses do we own? Innovation and restructuring our community starts with how and where we spend our money!

4. Several colleges and universities that feature a high African American enrollment also have extremely low graduation rates. A report released by the Education Trust organization in 2010 found only one in ten black students graduate in six years from Wayne State University, located in Detroit, Michigan.[29] We need to provide more support to our college students and better preparation for high school students. How can we

expect our students to be successful if we don't support or prepare them?

5. The so-called "Talented Tenth" or the intellectual and/ or wealthy class of African Americans appear disconnected from those who live in more dire conditions. Instead of reinvesting themselves into the community as black leaders did prior to and during the Civil Rights Movement, the "American Dream." My question to them is what if Martin Luther King pursued the American Dream instead of his dream? Where would you be?

When I think about all of the problems that plague our community, it would seem that having our own media outlet would help us address these issues in a constructive and widely effectively manner. Sadly, the television network known as Black Entertainment Television (BET) is in many ways a large contributor to the problems we see. With the erosion of television shows that depict an educated and positive African American family base, BET could have played a significant role in the development of future positive television shows. In large part, the problem we have is we allow the

Source: Joel Barbee

media and entertainers to constantly depict the negativity in our community without showing the positive outcomes that occur. When you watch BET and view the drama filled sitcoms, rap videos, and BET awards, please ask yourself, "Does this really describe everything we have to offer as a community?" Why doesn't BET feature more coverage of positive alternatives such as President Obama's family, African American history, minority research conferences, community outreach, interviews from successful black college graduates, etc. Why must we ALWAYS focus on the negative? We have black doctors,lawyers, CEOs, professors, accountants, nurses, business owners, and a black president. Instead of tailoring the network to depict all of the negative aspects of our culture, BET should work to promote the positive outcomes in order to change what we see in our community. **BET has clearly failed black America.**

As a teenager I remember watching a short segment titled "Channel 7 News Brightest and The Best" which featured top high school graduates who received scholarships to college. The problem is ALL of the students featured on this segment on this particular day were white. Despite maintaining an above average academic performance, I immediately asked my mother "Do black kids go to college?"

Do we care that our black men are incarcerated at such high rates? Do we care about the longer prison sentences black men are serving for crack cocaine offenses? How has the absence of a strong black man affected our community and/or your household? A few decades ago, the idea of a black man was synonymous with being a leader, educated, strong, fearless, and a servant of his people. Now being a black man is synonymous with crime, murder, dropout, incarceration, crack cocaine, and being absent from the household. How did we go from being influenced by Dr. Martin Luther King, to following the likes of "Lil Wayne"? Is Lil Wayne qualified to lead our people? Why do we pay attention to this non-sense? Are these rappers providing you with the means of escaping poverty and providing a better life for your family? Brothers and sisters *where did we go wrong?*

EMPLOYMENT

Employment: Last one in, First one out....WHY?

In the current economic climate, unemployment is a very sensitive yet critical issue in the black community. In 2008 I remember witnessing the erosion of employment in the neighborhood I grew up in. Nearly everyone I knew was unemployed and I could see the walls closing in on my job, as well. When General Motors and Chrysler filed bankruptcy in 2009 after laying off tens of thousands of employees, I knew a massive transition in the workforce was underway. It was at this time that I realized how dependent African Americans in Detroit were on jobs in the manufacturing sector and how detrimental the absence of such jobs would be to the community. For many African Americans in Detroit, the automotive industry provided stable employment at wages that made it possible to own cars, homes, and enjoy the typical middle class lifestyle. How would the absence of such a lucrative opportunity that African Americans in Detroit have depended heavily upon for decades impact future generations? It could be argued that the availability of such a lucrative alternative over the years has contributed to the lack of emphasis that many African Americans place on education. How do you convince students to pursue a college degree that provides a starting salary of $30,000, when he or she could graduate high school and earn a similar salary at the age of 18? With some factory workers reporting gross income in excess of $70,000 per year, we have to realize that the availability of employment in the auto industry has affected our commitment to education. Now that these jobs are not widely available, what will we do? How will a generation who has never had to pursue higher education and/or a college degree teach their children to pursue such endeavors?

The graph featured on the next page shows unemployment separated by race on a national level. In 2011, African Americans were unemployed at significantly higher rates than their White and Hispanic peers. Why are African Americans unemployed in such high numbers?

Annual Unemployment Rate Ages 16 and Older by Race/Ethnicity, 2011

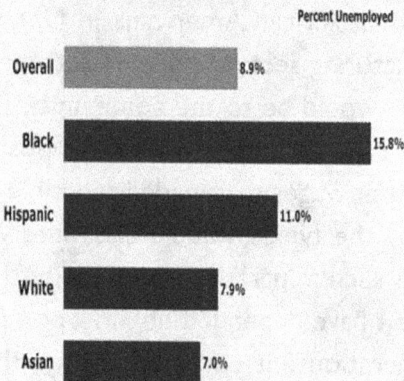

Percent Unemployed

Category	Percent Unemployed
Overall	8.9%
Black	15.8%
Hispanic	11.0%
White	7.9%
Asian	7.0%

NOTE: Data are not seasonally adjusted, with the exception of Asian workers.
SOURCE: Labor Force Statistics. Bureau of Labor Statistics. http://data.bls.gov/2012/cutdata.jsp?survey=ln. Accessed 1/20/12.

As I reflect on the education I received in school and at home, I realize that I was never taught how to find a job. Who taught you how to prepare for a job interview? Specifically, have you ever participated in a mock job interview at school or at home? Did anybody inform you of the expected attire, types of questions asked, appropriate responses to interview questions, what questions to ask in an interview, etc? If the answer is a clear "NO," we must admit that the absence of such preparation may play a critical role in this problem. Why isn't this information taught in public schools? Are good interview skills not as important as the subjects taught in our schools? It is very easy to place the blame on our parents, but we must remember that our parents received the same subpar education we received. Ideally, we would expect parents to provide their children with adequate preparation for finding a job, but how can a parent teach what he or she has never learned? We cannot expect working class families with subpar high school education to provide their children with the same preparation as middle class parents who have college degrees. Instead of pointing the blame at the school system or parents, I encourage educators to step up and fill the void. Am I blaming educators for not teaching students interview skills? NO! I am merely stating that we all see that we have an "employment" problem in the black community and it needs a solution. Let's fix it! **If parents and students are willing to learn,** *then educators should be willing to teach.* Will you help our children?

On the next few pages, line graphs show a consistent increase in unemployment in the United States and pie graphs depict overall unemployment in Michigan and Detroit as of December 2009. Including unemployed workers, discouraged, and part time workers who are actively seeking full-time employment, nearly twenty-five percent of the workforce in the U.S. is under-employed. Although the graph of Detroit shows "official" unemployment at twenty-seven percent, in 2009 Mayor David Bing stated true unemployment in Detroit was estimated to be "closer to fifty percent." Since many of my readers have direct and indirect experiences relating to unemployment, I will not belabor the urgency embedded in these statistics. However, I will ask where do we go from here? How did we get in this mess? How do we prevent this from happening again and/or prepare in case it does happen again? What would you have done differently if you had known you would be unemployed or under-employed? How are you preparing your children for the economic challenges they may face as adults?

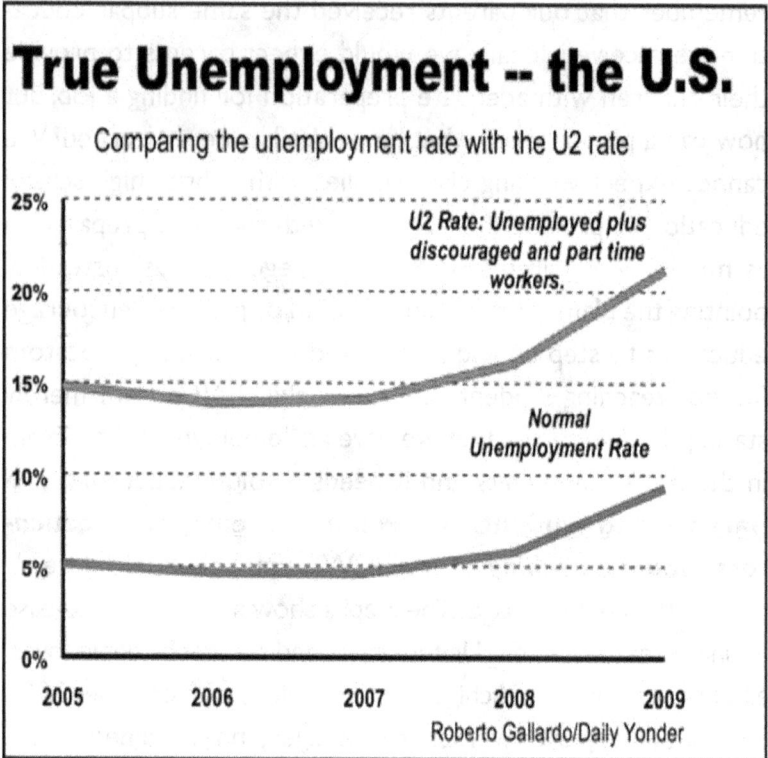

True Unemployment -- the U.S.

Comparing the unemployment rate with the U2 rate

U2 Rate: Unemployed plus discouraged and part time workers.

Normal Unemployment Rate

| 25% |
| 20% |
| 15% |
| 10% |
| 5% |
| 0% |

2005   2006   2007   2008   2009

Roberto Gallardo/Daily Yonder

Source: Roberto Gallardo, Southern Rural Development Center, Mississippi State University

Job woes hit Detroit harder

The Michigan unemployment rate is the highest in the nation, and worse in Detroit, approaching the 50 percent figure cited recently by Mayor Dave Bing.

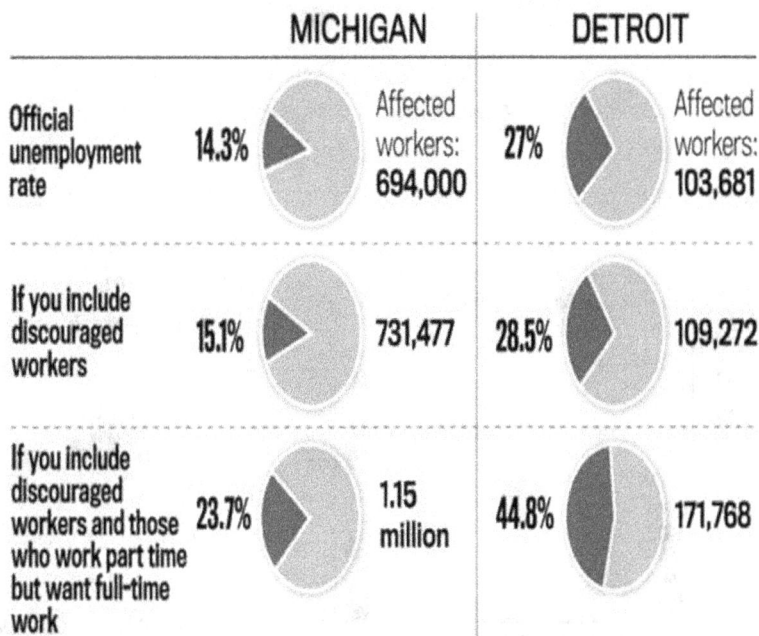

	MICHIGAN		DETROIT	
Official unemployment rate	**14.3%**	Affected workers: **694,000**	**27%**	Affected workers: **103,681**
If you include discouraged workers	**15.1%**	**731,477**	**28.5%**	**109,272**
If you include discouraged workers and those who work part time but want full-time work	**23.7%**	**1.15 million**	**44.8%**	**171,768**

Estimate based on Bureau of Labor Statistics' alternative measures of unemployment for 12-month period ending in September.

The Detroit News

Source: The Detroit News (2009)

Although the unemployment crisis emphasizes the need for higher education and job preparation courses, it is important to realize that equality is not guaranteed upon securing employment. According to Dr. Eric Grodsky, sociology professor at the University of Minnesota, and Dr. Devah Pager, sociology professor at Princeton University, "Despite the gains made by blacks in overcoming occupational segregation, however, black men's earnings continued to fall far short of the earnings of their white peers at all levels of economic attainment" (542).[30]

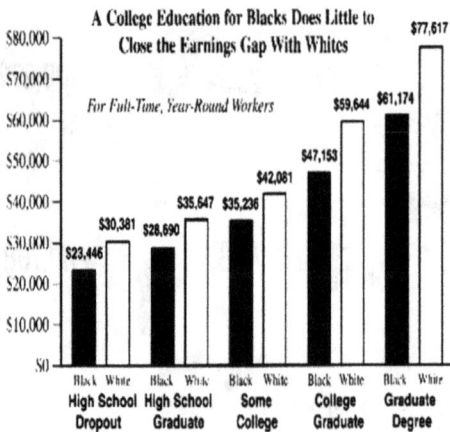

A College Education for Blacks Does Little to Close the Earnings Gap With Whites

For Full-Time, Year-Round Workers

	Black	White
High School Dropout	$23,446	$30,381
High School Graduate	$28,690	$35,547
Some College	$35,236	$42,081
College Graduate	$47,153	$59,644
Graduate Degree	$61,174	$77,617

Source: U.S. Census Bureau.

The graph on the left shows even when educational attainment is the same amongst black and white workers, whites earn considerably more.

Surprisingly, the income disparity actually increases as education attainment increases. Researchers have proposed multiple theories to explain the income disparity; however, each theory is flawed. For example, Drs. Grodsky and Pager stated the structural mobility theory emphasizes the disproportionate representation of African Americans in positions of lower status.[31] Yet, research shows that African Americans are represented in positions of high status, yet the income disparity persists. Why is there such a considerable difference in compensation when educational attainment is equal? Are we going to accept this? How do we address such inequality? What are the consequences of doing nothing?

In light of the dramatic increase in females who are obtaining higher education and the fact that females earn more degrees than men annually, I find it very interesting that an income disparity still exists. Surprisingly, the graph featured below follows the same trend as the disparity between black and white workers, with consistent increases in wage disparity as educational attainment increases. In fields such as academia, women not only earn less than their male counterparts despite equal education, they are less likely to reach full professorship.[31] Research shows from 1975 to 1994, the percentage of full-time female faculty members with tenure increased less than two percent (from 46% to 48%) while the percentage of male faculty with tenure increased eight percent (from 64% to 72%).[32] Although women earn nearly fifty percent of all PhDs granted in a single year, they represent only thirty-five percent of tenured or tenure-track faculty, and twenty-eight percent of full professors nationwide.[32,33] Sadly, these findings suggest that a "glass ceiling" still exists for women in some professions despite equal education.

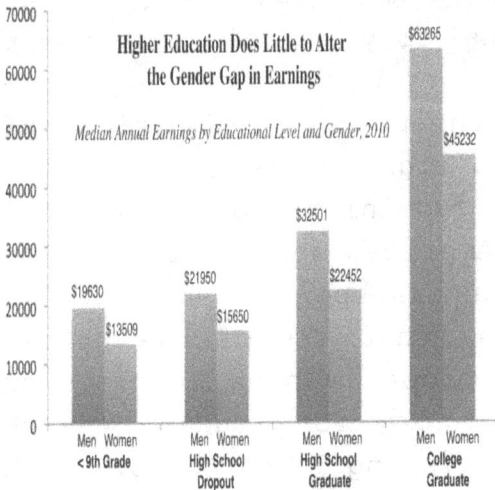

Higher Education Does Little to Alter the Gender Gap in Earnings

Median Annual Earnings by Educational Level and Gender, 2010

Educational Level	Men	Women
< 9th Grade	$19630	$13509
High School Dropout	$21950	$15650
High School Graduate	$32501	$22452
College Graduate	$63265	$45232

One major question that we must ask ourselves in regards to employment is WHERE ARE THE BLACK OWNED BUSINESSES? How much of our money stays in our community to help our schools, homes, and improve the services we receive?

The Detroit News

"At least one city school is visibly bearing the scars of the district's financial woes with an appeal for donations of toilet paper and light bulbs.

This week, administrators at the Academy of the Americas sent a letter home with students asking parents and others to donate items "that are of the utmost importance for proper school functioning and most importantly for student health and safety" – including light bulbs, trash bags, paper towel rolls and toilet paper. Students said the items were expected to be accepted at the front office starting Monday (The Detroit News, 2009)."[34]

Why do our neighborhoods look like war zones? Where is our money going? In the article "What Spending Half a Trillion Dollars on Hair Products says About Us," writer H. Fields Grenee states, "Consider this: $46,326 was the median household income in the United States according to 2010 U.S. Census data and the average income for African American families was $32,584, well below a middle-class lifestyle. Yet we over-spend for the purpose of appearance. Why is this?"[35] What sense does it make to have thousands of dollars invested in clothes, accessories, and entertainment, yet not have adequate housing or savings. Brothers and sisters where did we go wrong? First and foremost brothers and sisters, we must blame ourselves. We have to realize that we have allowed ourselves to be misled by the debt driven media. Corporate America promotes the idea that we should measure our happiness by the value of our materialistic possessions. Yet, what happens when you own every name brand pair of jeans and shoes or continue to purchase cars every three years but do not have sufficient savings for economic hardship? What happens if you lose your job? We all know this can happen and it has happened to some of us. Brothers and sisters after accepting the blame for our shortcomings, we must make the corrections necessary to ensure that our children do not repeat our mistakes.

In light of the increase in purchasing power in the African American community, the need for black-owned businesses has never been greater. I remember hearing several inspirational figures state the best investment an individual can make is in themselves. Brothers and sisters, the best investment we can make is in our future. Why do we wait on the government to create jobs when collectively we possess the financial means to create jobs? The problem is that we have allowed the "American Dream" to separate us from one another. Our households exemplify the greatest division in our community because the "black family" structure has been broken. For example, Dr. William Darity Jr, an African American studies professor at Duke University, and Dr. Samuel Myers, professor of Human Relations and Social Justice at the University of Minnesota, found the percentage of female-headed black households increased from 25% to 40% between 1965 and 1980.[36] Darity &

Myers also concluded that regardless of race, female-headed households are typically poor and considered part of the "permanent underclass." After investigating the increasing trend of African American female-headed households, Drs. Ross & Sawhill stated the courts have made AFDC (Aid to Families with Dependent Children or commonly known as "Welfare") the primary source of income for women who are not employed.[37] Have you ever considered how welfare has affected our community? Does welfare provide a means for our people to stay afloat in hard times or does it encourage our people to settle in life, remain comfortably poor, and dependent on such government support? By remaining dependent on such support, we fail to capitalize on opportunities to build businesses and the networks necessary to rebuild our neighborhoods and schools. In many ways AFDC is our problem. Will a child ever walk if you carry him or her every day? Welfare has carried us every day brothers and sisters and it is time for us to obtain employment and walk on our own. Brothers and sisters we can do better…for ourselves and for our children.

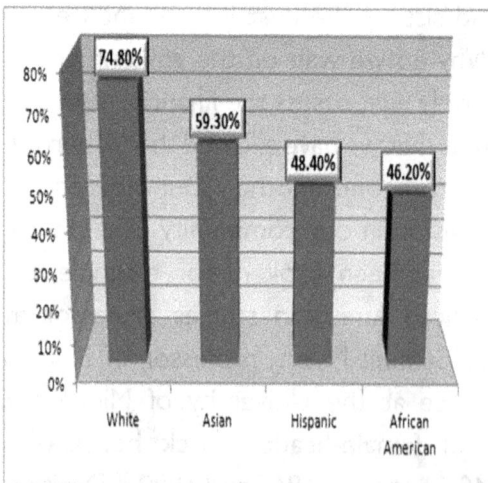

Source: U.S. Census Bureau 2010

Homeownership is one of the most important and lucrative ways Americans accumulate wealth, gain access to better neighborhoods, and access to better school systems. The graph featured below shows African Americans consistently lag behind their white counterparts in the percentage of homeownership. While overall homeownership in the United States is stated to be around 66%, the homeownership rate for African Americans in 2010 was 46.2%.[38] Since homeownership is such a critical way for us to accumulate wealth and the cost of homeownership is at its lowest point in several decades, why don't we own more homes? Where do we learn how to buy homes? I find it very interesting how we allow students to graduate from high school as if they are prepared to function independently in this society, yet they are not taught how to flourish in this society. While it is easy to blame parents for not teaching their children how to purchase homes, we must realize that many parents do not understand the fundamentals of this process. How can we expect a large majority of minorities to understand the complexities of homeownership when minorities in several states have endured decades of discrimination in the housing industry?

History of Housing Discrimination in America[39,40]

- History shows us that as far back as the 1600s, being black has been associated with restrictions on where an individual can obtain employment, live, and travel.
- The Civil Rights Act of 1875 provided that everyone, regardless of race, color, or previous condition of servitude, was entitled to the same treatment in "public accommodations"
- In 1883, The United States Supreme Court ruled that the Civil Rights Act of 1875, which forbid discrimination in hotels, trains, and other public avenues, was unconstitutional. This ruling in many ways justified legalized discrimination and fueled the rise of Jim Crow laws.
- The Jim Crow Laws, which were enforced between 1876 and 1965, mandated racial segregation in public facilities, with an emphasis on "separate but equal" for African Americans. During this time period it was considered "illegal" for African Americans to purchase land in "white zoned" areas.
- In the 1917 case of Buchanan v. Warley, the Supreme Court ruled that Louisville's housing discrimination practices violated the 14th Amendment's due protection clause because it interfered with private property sales between blacks and whites. Still, after this decision several states supported "legal" agreements between white homeowners to not sell or rent to racial minorities.
- The Civil Rights Act/Fair Housing Act of 1968 deemed all forms of housing discrimination unconstitutional

- The Equal Opportunity Act of 1974 made it illegal for any creditor to discriminate against an applicant on the basis of race, color, religion, gender, nationality, marital status, or age.
- The Community Re-investment Act of 1977 was implemented with the intentions of encouraging credit unions and banks to develop programs that met the demands of borrowers in their immediate vicinity.
- The Fair Housing Assistance Program of 1984 and Initiative Program of 1986 were implemented to aid in the processing of housing discrimination complaints.

Brothers and sisters we have accepted subpar conditions far too long in our community. We have accepted higher unemployment rates, over-reliance on government for monetary and food assistance, and unequal compensation for too long. How much longer will we depend on the government to do what we are capable of doing for ourselves? Our children need a holistic education that incorporates academics, employment related skills, and real world application. Education without application is DEAD! Will you accept these poor conditions? Will you accept higher unemployment rates as a consequence of being black in America? In the Civil Rights Era, the government promised equality. Do you see equality in the statistics presented? Instead of equality, I see a system that has permitted us to live "comfortably poor" and has appeased us just as a pacifier quiets a teething child. The time for being silent and satisfied is over. We must engage in ACTIVISM now!

POLITICAL ABSENTEEISM

Political Absenteeism: It's Time to Vote....Where are my Brothers and Sisters?

After reading the education, incarceration, and employment sections of this book, the importance of politics in our history and our daily lives should be recognized. By maintaining a strong presence in the political arena, African Americans have gained many of the rights that were not immediately given to us. Taking into consideration the struggle of the Civil Rights Movement and the fact that African Americans still do not receive adequate local services, I find it shocking that African Americans do not vote in large numbers and are not more active in politics. U.S. Census data from the year 2000 shows there were twenty-eight million African Americans who were within the voting age (18+ years of age), but only about 13 million African Americans voted in the 2004 presidential election.[41,42] Roughly 15 million African American voters, representing 53% of the eligible African American voting base, did not participate.

Why is there such a low turnout from African Americans at presidential elections? One important issue that attracts relatively little attention from the media is the impact of regulations that prevent felons from voting. Even though the laws that prevent felons from voting do not directly target a specific race, they certainly have a disproportionate impact on the African American community. Research shows an estimated

4.7 million people have been banned from voting due to a felony incarceration.[43] Nearly 40% of the felons who are disenfranchised are African American men.[44,45] Several researchers have proposed that high minority incarceration rates throughout the last several decades could be a major reason that felony voting bans were initially imposed and remain in our society today. Should individuals who were convicted of felony offenses be banned from voting for their entire lives?

Another important factor that could contribute to the low African American turnout at election polls is the historical context that denied African Americans the right to vote. Our ancestors encountered every form of voter discrimination and some lost their lives for the sake of voting. Below is a chronological depiction of the struggle African Americans endured during their quest for the right to vote.

The Right to Vote[46,47,48]

- The 14th Amendment, ratified July 9th, 1868, extended U.S. citizenship to African Americans by stating, "Individuals born or naturalized in the United States are American citizens, including those born as slaves." This Amendment was proposed to nullify the decision rendered in the Dred Scott Case in 1857, which ruled that African Americans were not citizens

- The 15th Amendment of the U.S. Constitution, ratified February 3rd, 1870, granted African American **men** the right to vote by stating "The right of citizens of the United States to vote shall not be denied or abridged by the United States or by any state on account of race, color, or previous condition of servitude." Notice that women were **NOT** included in this Amendment.

- In 1871 Georgia implemented the use of a "poll tax" to discourage African Americans from voting. The poll tax, which required voters to pay ALL back taxes before they were allowed to vote, was estimated to have reduced African American turnout by as much as fifty percent.

- In 1882 South Carolina adopted the first "literacy test" in order to discourage African Americans from voting. Voters were required to place ballots for different electoral positions in separate boxes. If a ballot were placed in the wrong box it was thrown out. Also, the boxes were continuously rearranged in order to prevent literate individuals from aiding illiterate individuals. Such practices had a tremendous negative impact on African Americans because at this time, an estimated 40-60% were illiterate compared, to only 8-18% of their white counterparts.

- In 1873 one hundred African Americans, who were gathered to defend Republican officeholders, were murdered by an angry white mob. The U.S. Supreme Court dismissed the indictment in the 1875 case of U.S. v Cruikshank, thus freeing the men who were indicted.

- Between 1880 and 1901, several Southern states engaged in a practice called "electoral fraud" by throwing out Republican votes or counting them in favor of the Democrats despite selection of the contrary. Two inspectors in the Kentucky election were indicted, due to their refusal to count black votes in the city election. The Supreme Court dismissed the indictment in the 1875 case of U.S. v Reese.

- The 19th Amendment, ratified August 18th, 1920, extended voting rights to women.

- In 1923 Texas passed a law that banned African Americans from participating in Democratic primary elections. In the case of Nixon v. Herndon (1927), the Supreme Court overturned this law due to a clear violation of the 14th and 15th Amendments. Immediately afterwards Texas passed another law that permitted each party's executive committee to determine who could vote in the primary election. The Texas Democratic Executive Committee proceeded to ban blacks from participating in the primary election.

- The Voting Rights Act, ratified August 6, 1965, banned all the discriminatory tactics, such as literacy tests, poll taxes, and other requirements that were used to disenfranchise black voters.

- In the 2008 presidential election, the Republican National Committee agreed to use mortgage foreclosure lists to challenge the eligibility of voters. A study conducted by Michigan's Department of Labor and Growth found that more than 60% of the subprime housing loans in Michigan were made for African Americans. Research has consistently shown that African Americans overwhelmingly cast votes in favor of the Democratic Party. A class action law suit was filed by the Democratic National Committee, which resulted in Republicans denying these allegations and the case was dismissed with prejudice.

Although the struggle our ancestors endured to obtain and maintain the right to vote is an important reason for our participation in political events, the poor services we currently receive should be an even greater motivating factor. In early 2012, the police department in Detroit, Michigan implemented a new response system called "Virtual 911." In regards to this new system, on March 6th, 2012 the myfox2detroit.com website reported,

"An old man beaten down by a carjacker last month. People stepping around him like he's garbage. Ignoring his calls for help. But what if somebody had the heart to call the police? There's a distinct possibility they wouldn't have come. Not with the new 911 policy. Unknown to most people, the Detroit police last week quietly rolled out its latest plan to save money: Virtual 911. This is how it works. If you've been held up and the gunman is long gone, or you've been assaulted but not too badly, or your home has been broken into,

that's not 911 anymore. They'll transfer you or you can call the Telephone Crime Reporting Unit yourself at 313-267-4600."

The implementation of Virtual 911 would lead to the closing of ALL Detroit Police Stations at 4:00 P.M. on a daily basis. Upon receiving news of this new system, I immediately wrote a letter, which is located on page **sixty-one** to the Detroit Police Chief Ralph Godbee Jr. and City Councilman Kenneth Cockrel to voice my disapproval. In a city that consistently ranks as one of the most dangerous cities in America, I find it absolutely ridiculous that ALL the police stations would be closed at 4:00 P.M. Brothers and sisters why do we accept these poor conditions? What other city in America has a high crime rate and ZERO police stations open after 4:00 P.M.? This is unacceptable, and we must address this NOW! The lives of our brothers, sisters, and children are at stake.

If you are wondering how bad things are in Detroit, you will not need to look any further. I remember visiting my grandmother, who lives on the west side of Detroit, in mid-2011 and hearing the story of an older gentleman who needed ambulatory services but was denied. According to several spectators of this event, this particular gentleman was working under his car when the tire device broke causing the car to fall on top of him. Immediately, family members came to his aid to lift the vehicle off of him and a call requesting ambulatory services was placed. In response to their request, they were told, "There are no ambulances in service in your area. He must be transported to the hospital via car." Brothers and sisters how in the HELL are there no ambulances available in the areas we live in? How much more of this are we going to take? The police do not respond to calls in our neighborhoods, police stations are closing at 4pm, and some serious emergency calls placed to 911 are being transferred to a "hotline," instead of the police. I HAVE HAD ENOUGH! It is time we take control of our lives and our city. Do your City Council members talk to you to find out your needs? Why do we vote for these "imaginary leaders" who we have never seen active in our community? Why don't we encourage a proven leader or activist in our community (i.e. teacher, mentor, etc.) to run for office? Why don't you run for office? We need passionate leaders who believe in our children and are able to adapt to the demands of TODAY. To put it bluntly, brothers and sisters, some of the members of city council HAVE TO GO!

After exploring research in education, incarceration, employment, homeownership, and political activism, I hope my deep interests in community activism and education reform are recognized. We have to admit that our society has evolved much faster than our education system, and our current standards of proficiency are no longer acceptable due to the increased demands society places on its workers. Today, we need more information at a much faster rate and therefore, the preparation for adult life needs to be commensurate with the expectations we have for our students. The numerous technological advances of today and the severe consequences of falling behind stress the need for improvements in our education system. I firmly believe improvements in our education system will, in turn, decrease incarceration rates and increase positive outcomes, such as the establishment of more black owned businesses. By taking our children's future seriously, our children will begin to take their lives seriously. We cannot tell our children they can be doctors, lawyers, and business owners and give them deficient supplies to accomplish those goals. **Brothers and Sisters, we have to make a choice.** Either we can work together and progress with this society, or we can do nothing and watch as economic conditions worsen and our children become victims of this system. Please turn the page, complete the survey, and send your responses to the specified email address. Brothers and sisters I am tired of seeing our community suffer! Will you stand with me brothers and sisters? Will you walk with me?

QUESTIONNAIRE

1. If you graduated from Detroit Public Schools, are you satisfied with the preparation you received for college?

2. If you are not satisfied, what changes would you like to see Detroit Public Schools make?

3. What additional courses should Detroit Public Schools offer?

4. Do you approve of how the Detroit Police Department handles crime in the community?

5. Do you approve of the work City Council Members do in the community?

6. What additional ideas do you have to improve our educational system and increase positive outcomes?

Please visit www.weneedchange.org

Submit all responses to charlesbell@weneedchange.org

If Michigan Works can provide free job preparatory courses/training, why can't Detroit Public Schools?

Kenneth V. Cockrel, Jr.

President of Detroit City Council
1340 Coleman A. Young Municipal Center
2 Woodward Ave.
Detroit, MI 48226

March 13, 2012

Dear Councilman:

I am writing this letter to express my deep dissatisfaction with
the subpar services the city of Detroit provides to its citizens.
As a near lifelong resident of Detroit, I relocated to Lansing MI
in 2008 to pursue my master's degree and gain the skills necessary to serve my people. Despite my departure from the city, I
made it a priority to remain informed on the issues that affect
Detroit. I am deeply dissatisfied with the implementation of
the new "Virtual 911" system the Detroit Police Department
are using because at best it is a poor method for managing
crime and a poor example of leadership on the behalf of city
officials. How can you expect people to move back to Detroit
if the police force cannot provide adequate protection to its
citizens? Protecting citizens from violent criminals needs to
be the number ONE priority in the city and if Detroit police
officers are unable to accomplish this task city officials need to
DO SOMETHING!!! Ask for help from the state police, FBI, or
the governor. WE NEED HELP!!!

As of 3-6-2012 the myfoxdetroit.com website states, "An old man beaten down by a carjacker last month. People stepping around him like he's garbage. Ignoring his calls for help. But what if somebody had the heart to call the police? <u>There's a distinct possibility they wouldn't have come. Not with the new 911 policy.</u> Unknown to most people, the Detroit police last week quietly rolled out its latest plan to save money: Virtual 911. This is how it works. <u>If you've been held up and the gunman is long gone, or you've been assaulted but not too badly, or your home has been broken into, that's not 911 anymore. They'll transfer you or you can call the Telephone Crime Reporting Unit yourself at 313-267-4600.</u>

I am writing this letter to inform you that this is UNACCEPTABLE! City Council must do better! Councilman Cockrel…your actions will not be forgotten on Election Day.

Sincerely,

Charles Bell

QUOTES/INTELLECTUAL THOUGHTS

"If this is going to be a Christian nation that doesn't help the poor, either we have to pretend that Jesus was just as selfish as we are, or we've got to acknowledge that He commanded us to love the poor and serve the needy without condition and then admit that we just don't want to do it."
Stephen Colbert

A nation that continues year after year to spend more money on military defense than on programs of social uplift is approaching spiritual doom.
Dr. Martin Luther King Jr.

I didn't know I was a slave until I found out I couldn't do the things I wanted.
Frederick Douglass

If there is no struggle, there is no progress.
Frederick Douglass

I would like to be remembered as a person who wanted to be free....so other people would also be free
Rosa Parks

I submit to you that if a man hasn't discovered something
that he will die for, he isn't fit to live
Dr. Martin Luther King, Jr.

"I always tried so hard to fit in, and then I figured out that
I didn't want to fit."
Anthony Davis

The only thing more expensive than education is
ignorance."
Benjamin Franklin

"Successful people don't have fewer problems. They have
determined that nothing will stop them from going forward."
Dr. Benjamin Carson

WORKS CITED

1. American Civil Liberties Union. Cracks in the System: Twenty Years of the Unjust Federal Crack Cocaine . 2006. Web. <http://www.aclu.org/pdfs/drugpolicy/cracksinsystem_20061025.pdf>.

2. Anderson, Veronica. "Catalyst Chicago." Lopsided Discipline Takes Toll on Black Male Students. Catalyst in Depth, 2009. Web. 20 Jun 2012. <http://www.catalyst-chicago.org/sites/catalyst-chicago.org/files/assets/20090619/catalystmayjun09.pdf>.

3. Angeli, David. "A Second Look at Crack Cocaine Sentencing Policies: One More Try on Federal Equal Protection." American Criminal Law Review. 34. (1997): 1211-1239. Print.

4. Austin, Algernon. Reversal of fortune: Economic Gains of 1990s Overturned for African Americans from 2000-07. Economic Policy Institute, 18092008. Web. 20 Jun 2012. <http://www.epi.org/publication/bp220/>.

5. Behrens, Angela, Christopher Uggen, et al. "Ballot Manipulation and the 'Menace of Negro Domination: Racial Threat and Felon Disenfranchisement in the United States, 1850-2002." American Journal of Sociology. 109. (2003): 559-605. Print.

6. Big Gaps Small Gaps in Serving African American Students. The Education Trust, 09082010. Web. 21 Jun

2012. <http://www.edtrust.org/sites/edtrust.org/files/publications/files/CRO Brief-AfricanAmerican.pdf>.

7. Brand-Williams, Oralandar, Mark Hicks, et al. "DPS Academy Issues Plea for Toilet Paper." Detroit News [Detroit] 08 01 2009, Web. 21 Jun. 2012. < http://www.detroitnews.com/article/20090108/SCHOOLS/901080424>.

8. Chin, Gabriel, and Randy Wagner. "The Tyranny of the Minority: Jim Crow and the Counter-Majoritarian Difficulty." Harvard Civil Rights-Civil Liberties Law Review. 43. (2006): 65-125. Print.

9. Children's Defense Fund. School suspensions: Are They Helping Children?. Washington: Children's Defense Fund, 1975. Print.

10. Collins, W., Eleanor Maccoby, et al. "Contemporary Research on Parenting. The Case for Nature and Nurture." American Psychologist. 55. (2000): 218-232. Print.

11. Cross, Theodore. "Special Report: The Ominous Gender Gap in African American Higher Education." Journal of Blacks in Higher Education. 23. (1999): 6-9. Print.

12. Cummings, Melbourne. "The Changing Image of the Black Family on Television." Journal of Popular Culture. 22.2 (1988): 75-85. Print.

13. Darity, William, and Samuel Myers. "Exploring Black Welfare are Dependency Changes in Black Family Structure: Implications for Welfare Dependency." American Economic Review. 73. (1983): 59-64. Print.

14. Dunn, Lloyd. "Special Education for the Mildly Retarded. Is Much of it Justifiable?." *Exceptional Children*. 23. (1968): 5-21. Print.

15. Feagin, Joe. "Excluding Blacks and Others From Housing: The Foundation of White racism." Cityscape. 4 (1999): 79-91. Web. 20 Jun. 2012. <http://www.huduser.org/periodicals/cityscpe/vol4num3/ feagin.pdf>.

16. Feagin, Joe, and Clairece Feagin. Racial and Ethnic Relations. 6th. Upper Saddle River: Prentice-Hall, 1998. Print.

17. Fellner, Jamie, and Marc Mauer. The Sentencing Project and Human Rights Watch. Losing the Vote: The Impact of Felony Disenfranchisement Laws in the United States. Washington, D.C.: 1998. Print.

18. Fletcher, George. "Disenfranchisement as Punishment: Reflection on the Racial Uses of Infamia." UCLA Law Review. 46. (1999): 1895-1908. Print.

19. Ford, Laurie, Tori Kearns, et al. "African American Students Representation in Special Education Programs." Journal of Negro Education. 4. (2005): 297-310. Print.

20. Gregory, Ann, and Pharmicia Mosely. "The Discipline Gap: Teachers Views on the Over-representation of African American Students in the Discipline System." Equity & Excellence in Education. 37. (2004): 18-30. Print.

21. Grenee, H. Fields. What Spending A Half A Trillion Dollars on Hair Care and Weaves Says About Us. Madamenoire, 11052011. Web. 24 Jun 2012. <http://madamenoire.com/57134/what-spending-a-half-

a-trillion-dollars-on-hair-care-and-weaves-says-about-us/>.

22. Grodsky, Eric, and Devah Pager. "The Structure of Disadvantage:Individual and Occupational Determinants of the Black-White Wage Gap." American Sociological Review. 66. (2001): 542-567. Print.

23. Given Half a Chance: The Schott 50 States Report on Public Education and Black Males. 29.Scott Foundation for Public Education, 2008. Web. 20 Jun 2012. <http://www.blackboysreport.org/>.

24. Harvey, Alice. "Ex-Felon Disenfranchisement and its Influence on the Black Vote" The Need for a Second Look." University of Pennsylvania Law Review. 142. (1994): 1145-1189. Print.

25. Higgins, Lori. "Schools' Discipline of Special-ed Students -- Particularly Black Ones -- Raises Concerns." Detroit Free Press [Detroit] 12 06 2012, Web. 21 Jun. 2012. <http://www.freep.com/article/20120612/NEWS06/206120431/Schools-discipline-of-special-ed-students-particularly-black-ones-raises-concerns>.

26. Holder, Kelly. U.S. Census Bureau Current Population Reports. Voting and Registration in the Election of November 2004. Web. <http://www.census.gov/prod/2006pubs/p20 –556.pdf>.

27. Housing and Household Economic Statistics Divison. U.S. Census Bureau, n.d. Web. 21 Jun 2012. <http://www.census.gov/hhes/www/housing/census/historic/ownershipbyrace.html>.

28. Hutchinson, Earl. Why 8 Million African Americans Are Not Registered to Vote. New American Media, 07102008. Web. 24 Jun 2012. <http://news.newameri-

camedia.org/news/view_article.html?article_id=c2259
8f2e13ed9421a7933e8d9d25977>.

29. Kolodner, Meredith, and . "Study Shows rich-poor gap in New York." New York Daily News [New York] 12 10 2010, Web. 21 Jun. 2012. <http://articles.nydailynews. com/2010-10-12/local/27077923_1_rich-poor-gap-school-district-funding-poor-districts>.

30. Kousser, Joseph The Shaping of Southern Politics: Suffrage Restriction and the Establishment of the One-Party South, 1880-1910. 1st ed. New Haven: Yale University, 1974. Print.

31. Kunjufu, Jawanza. Keeping Black Boys out of Special Education. Chicago: African American Images, 2005. Print.

32. Mauer, Marc, and Tracy Huling. Sentencing Project. Young black Americans and the Criminal Justice System: Five years later. Washington, D.C.: Sentencing Project, 1995. Print.

33. Mendez, Linda, Howard Knoff, et al. "School Demographic Variables and out of School Suspension Rates: A Quantitative and Qualitative Analysis of a Large, Ethnically Diverse School District." Psychology in the Schools. 3. (2002): 259-277. Print.

34. National Center for Education Statistics. (2005a). Postsecondary institutions in the United States: Fall 2003 and Degrees and Other Awards Conferred: 2002-03 (NCES 2005-154). Washington, DC: Author.

35. National Center for Education Statistics. (2005b). Integrated Postsecondary Education Data System (IPEDS), Winter 2003-04, Table 228. Washington, DC: Author.

36. . National Association of School Psychologists Online. National Association of School Psychologists, 2005. Web. 20 Jun 2012. <http://www.nasponline.org/resources/culturalcompetence/minority_demog.asp

37. Nixon v. Condon. Disenfrachisement of the Negro in Texas. New Haven: 1932. Print.

38. Oswald, Donald, Martha Coutinho, et al. "Ethnic Representation in Special Education." Journal of Special Education. 32. (1999): 194-206. Print.

39. Patton,James."The Disproportionate Representation of African Americans in Special Education: Looking Behind the Curtain for Understanding and Solutions." Journal of Special Education. 32. (1998): 25-31. Print.

40. Petersilia, Joan (2005). "From Cell to Society: Who Is Returning Home?." In Prisoner Reentry and Crime in America, ed. Jeremy Travis and Christy Visher, pp. 15–49. New York: Cambridge University Press.

41. Recording Industry of America Database. Recording Industry Association of America, n.d. Web. 21 Jun 2012. <http://www.riaa.com/>.

42. Ross, Heather and Sawhill, Isabel, Time of Transition: The Growth of Families Headed by Women, Washington, 1975. Print.

43. Saulny, Susan. "Study on Special Education Finds Low Graduation Rate." New York Times [New York] 03 06 2005, Web. 21 Jun. 2012. <http://www.nytimes.com/2005/06/03/education/03dropout.html>.

44. Shapiro, Andrew. "Challenging Criminal Disenfranchisement Under the Voting Rights Act: A

New Strategy." Yale Law Journal. 103. (1993): 537-566. Print.

45. Skiba, Russell, Robert Michael, Abra Nardo, et al. "The Color of Discipline: Sources of Racial and Gender Disproportionality in School Punishment." (2000): 1-26. Web. 20 Jun. 2012. <http://pcfly.info/pdf/COD/7. pdf>.

46. The Kaiser Family Foundation, Kaiser Fast Facts. Data Source: Force Statistics. Bureau of Labor Statistics. accessed on April 1, 2012, available at http://data.bls. gov/PDQ/outside.jsp?survey=ln

47. Tolan, Patrick, Deborah Gorman-Smith, et al. "The Developmental Ecology of Urban Males' Youth Violence." Developmental Psychology. 39. (2003): 274-291. Print.

48. Topper, Greg. "The Face of the American Teacher: White and Female, While her Students are Ethnically Diverse." USA Today 02 06 2003. Web. 20 Jun. 2012. <http://www.usatoday.com/educate/college/education/articles/20030706.htm>.

49. U.S. Department of Commerce, Bureau of the United States. Census of the United States. Washing, D.C.: Government Printing Office, Print.

50. Uggen, Christopher, and Jeff Manza. "Democratic Contraction? The Political Consequences of Felon Disenfranchisement in the United States." American Sociological Review. 67. (2002): 777-803. Print.

51. U.S. Department of Education, National Center for Education Statistics, Higher Education General Information Survey (HEGIS), "Degrees and Other Formal Awards Conferred" surveys, 1976-77 and

1980-81; and 1989-90 through 2008-09 Integrated Postsecondary Education Data System, "Completions Survey" (IPEDS-C:90-99), and Fall 2000 through Fall 2009. (This table was prepared September 2010.)

52. U.S. Department of Education, National Center for Education Statistics, Integrated Postsecondary Education Data System (IPEDS), Winter 2005-06, Winter 2007-08, and Winter 2009-10, Human Resources component, Fall Staff section.

53. U.S.Department of Justice. Bureau of Justice Statistics. Prison and Jail Inmates Midyear 2007. Washington, D.C.: 2008. Print.

54. Visher, Christy, Sara Debus, et al. American Policy Center. Employment After Prison: A Longitudinal Study of Releasees in Three States. Urban Institute, 2008. Web. <http://www.urban.org/UploadedPDF/411778_employment_after_prison.pdf>.

55. Ward, L., Edwina Hansbrough, et al. "Contributions of Music Video Exposure to Black Adolescents Gender and Sexual Schemas." Journal of Adolescence Research. 20. (2005): 143-166. Print.

56. West, Heather, and William Sabol. "Prisoners in 2007." Bureau of Justice Statistics, 2008. Web. 20 Jun 2012. <http://bjs.ojp.usdoj.gov/index.cfm?ty=pbdetail&iid=903>.

57. West, Martha. "Women Faculty: Frozen In Time." Academe. 81.4 (1995): 26-29. Print.

58. West, Martha, and John Curtis. AAUP Faculty Gender Equity Indicators 2006. American Association of University Professors, 2006. Web. 24 Jun 2012. <http://www.aaup.org/NR/rdonlyres/63396944-

44BE-4ABA-9815-5792D93856F1/0/AAUPGenderEquityIndicators2006.pdf>.

59. Williams, Lea. Servants of the People: The 1960s Legacy of African American Leadership. 2nd. Greensboro: Palgrave Macmillan, 2008. 0-320. Print.

60. Wingood, Gina, Ralph DiClemente, et al. "A Longitudinal Study of Exposure to Rap Music Videos and Female Adolescents' Health." American Journal of Public Health. 93. (2003): 437-439. Print.

61. Wu, Shi-Chan. "Student Suspension: A Critical Reappraisal." Urban Review. 4. (1982): 254-303. Print.

62. Yinger, John. "Housing Discrimination and Residential Segregation." Focus. 21.2 (2000): 51-55. Web. 20 Jun. 2012. <http://www.irp.wisc.edu/publications/focus/pdfs/foc212.pdf>.

END NOTES

1. Cross, Theodore. "Special Report: The ominous gender gap in African American higher education." Journal of Blacks in Higher Education. 23. (1999): 6-9. Print

2. National Center for Education Statistics. (2005a). Postsecondary institutions in the UnitedStates: Fall 2003 and degrees and other awards conferred: 2002-03 (NCES 2005-154). Washington, DC: Author.

3. Given half a chance: The Schott 50 states report on public education and Black males. 29. Scott Foundation for Public Education, 2008. Web. 20 Jun 2012. <http://www.blackboysreport.org/>.

4. Dunn, Lloyd. "Special education for the mildly retarded. Is much of it justifiable?." Exceptional Children. 23. (1968): 5-21. Print.

5. Patton, James. "The disproportionate representation of African Americans in special education: Looking behind the curtain for understanding and solutions." Journal of Special Education. 32. (1998): 25-31. Print.

6. Kunjufu, Jawanza. Keeping black boys out of special education. Chicago: African American Images, 2005. Print.

7. National Association of School Psychologists Online. National Association of School Psychologists, 2005. Web. 20 Jun 2012. <http://www.nasponline.org/resources/culturalcompetence/minority_demog.asp

8. Topper, Greg. "The face of the American teacher: White and female, while her students are ethnically diverse." USA Today 02 06 2003. Web. 20 Jun. 2012.

9. Ford, Laurie, Tori Kearns, et al. "African American students representation in special education programs." Journal of Nego Education. 4. (2005): 297-310. Print.

10. Oswald, Donald, Martha Coutinho, et al. "Ethnic representation in special education." Journal of Special Education. 32. (1999): 194-206. Print.

11. Higgins, Lori. "Schools' discipline of special-ed students -- particularly black ones -- raises concerns." Detroit Free Press [Detroit] 12 06 2012, Web. 21 Jun. 2012.

12. Saulny, Susan. "Study on Special Education Finds Low Graduation Rate." New York Times [New York] 03 06 2005, Web. 21 Jun. 2012. <http://www.nytimes.com/2005/06/03/education/03dropout.html>.

13. Children's Defense Fund. School suspensions: Are they helping children?. Washington: Children's Defense Fund, 1975. Print.

14. Anderson, Veronica. "Catalyst Chicago." Lopsided discipline takes toll on black male students. Catalyst in Depth, 2009. Web. 20 Jun 2012. <http://www.catalyst-chicago.org/sites/catalyst-chicago.org/files/assets/20090619/catalystmayjun09.pdf>.

15. Wu, Shi-Chan. "Student Suspension: A critical reappraisal." Urban Review. 4. (1982): 254-303. Print.

16. Collins, W., Eleanor Maccoby, et al. "Contemporary research on parenting. The case for nature and nurture." American Psychologist. 55. (2000): 218-232. Print.

17. Skiba, Russell, Robert Michael, Abra Nardo, et al. "The color of discipline: Sources of racial and gender

disproportionality in school punishment.." (2000): 1-26. Web. 20 Jun. 2012. <http://pcfly.info/pdf/COD/7. pdf>.

18. Gregory, Ann, and Pharmicia Mosely. "The discipline gap: Teachers views on the over-representation of African American students in the discipline system." Equity & Excellence in Education. 37. (2004): 18-30. Print.

19. Kolodner, Meredith, and . "Study shows rich-poor gap in New York." New York Daily News [New York] 12 10 2010, Web. 21 Jun. 2012. <http://articles.nydailynews. com/2010-10-12/local/27077923_1_rich-poor-gap-school-district-funding-poor-districts>

20. Mendez, Linda, Howard Knoff, et al. "School demographic variables and out of school suspension rates: A quantitative and qualitative analysis of a large, ethnically diverse school district." Psychology in the Schools. 3. (2002): 259-277. Print.

21. Mauer, Marc, and Tracy Huling. Sentencing Project. Young black Americans and the criminal justice system: Five years later. Washington, D.C.: Sentencing Project, 1995. Print.

22. West, Heather, and William Sabol. "Prisoners in 2007." . Bureau of Justice Statistics, 2008. Web. 20 Jun 2012. <http://bjs.ojp.usdoj.gov/index. cfm?ty=pbdetail&iid=903>.

23. Angeli, David. "A second look at crack cocaine sentencing policies: One more try on federal equal protection." American Criminal Law Review. 34. (1997): 1211-1239. Print.

24. American Civil Liberties Union. 39. Cracks in the System: Twenty Years of the Unjust Federal Crack

Cocaine . 2006. Web. <http://www.aclu.org/pdfs/drug-policy/cracksinsystem_20061025.pdf>.

25. Williams, Lea. Servants of the People: The 1960s legacy of African American leadership. 2nd. Greenesboro: Palgrave Macmillan, 2008. 0-320. Print.

26. Recording Industry of America Database. Recording Industry Association of America, n.d. Web. 21 Jun 2012. <http://www.riaa.com/>.

27. Wingood, Gina, Ralph DiClemente, et al. "A longitudinal study of exposure to rap music videos and female adolescents' health." American Journal of Public Health. 93. (2003): 437-439. Print.

28. Ward, L., Edwina Hansbrough, et al. "Contributions of music video exposure to black adolescents gender and sexual schemas." Journal of Adolescence Research. 20. (2005): 143-166. Print.

29. Big Gaps Small Gaps in Serving African American Students. The Education Trust, 09082010. Web. 21 Jun 2012. <http://www.edtrust.org/sites/edtrust.org/files/publications/files/CRO Brief-AfricanAmerican.pdf>.

30. Grodsky, Eric, and Devah Pager. "The structure of disadvantage: Individual and occupational determinants of the black-white wage gap." American Sociological Review. 66. (2001): 542-567. Print.

31. West, Martha. "Women faculty: Frozen in time." Academe. 81.4 (1995): 26-29. Print.

32. U.S. Department of Education, National Center for Education Statistics, Higher Education General Information Survey (HEGIS), "Degrees and Other Formal Awards Conferred" surveys, 1976-77 and

1980-81; and 1989-90 through 2008-09 Integrated Postsecondary Education Data System, "Completions Survey" (IPEDS-C:90-99), and Fall 2000 through Fall 2009. (This table was prepared September 2010.)

33. West, Martha, and John Curtis. AAUP Faculty Gender Equity Indicators 2006. American Association of University Professors, 2006. Web. 24 Jun 2012. <http://www.aaup.org/NR/rdonlyres/63396944-44BE-4ABA-9815-5792D93856F1/0/AAUPGenderEquityIndicators2006.pdf>.

34. Brand-Williams, Oralandar, Mark Hicks, et al. "DPS academy issues plea for toilet paper." Detroit News [Detroit] 08 01 2009, n. pag. Web. 21 Jun. 2012. <http://www.detroitnews.com/article/20090108/SCHOOLS/901080424>.

35. Grenee, H. Fields. What Spending A Half A Trillion Dollars on Hair Care and Weaves Says About Us. Madamenoire, 11052011. Web. 24 Jun 2012. <http://madamenoire.com/57134/what-spending-a-half-a-trillion-dollars-on-hair-care-and-weaves-says-about-us/>.

36. Darity, William, and Samuel Myers. "Exploring black welfare are dependency changes in black family structure: Implications for welfare dependency." American Economic Review. 73. (1983): 59-64. Print.

37. Ross, Heather and Sawhill, Isabel, Time of Transition: The Growth of Families Headed by Women, Washington, 1975. Print.

38. Housing and Household Economic Statistics Divison. U.S. Census Bureau, n.d. Web. 21 Jun 2012. <http://

www.census.gov/hhes/www/housing/census/historic/ownershipbyrace.html>.

39. Yinger, John. "Housing discrimination and residential segregation as." Focus. 21.2 (2000): 51-55. Web. 20 Jun. 2012. <http://www.irp.wisc.edu/publications/focus/pdfs/foc212.pdf>.

40. Feagin, Joe. "Excluding blacks and others from housing: The foundation of white racism." Cityscape. 4 (1999): 79-91. Web. 20 Jun. 2012. <http://www.huduser.org/periodicals/cityscpe/vol4num3/ feagin.pdf>.

41. Holder, Kelly. U.S. Census Bureau Current Population Reports. Voting and registration in the election of November 2004. Web. <http://www.census.gov/prod/2006pubs/p20 –556.pdf>.

42. Hutchinson, Earl. Why 8 Million African Americans Are Not Registered to Vote. New American Media, 07102008. Web. 24 Jun 2012. <http://news.newameri-camedia.org/news/view_article.html?article_id=c2259 8f2e13ed9421a7933e8d9d25977>.

43. Fellner, Jamie, and Marc Mauer. The Sentencing Project and Human Rights Watch. Losing the vote: The impact of felony disenfranchisement laws in the United States. Washington, D.C.: 1998. Print.

44. Shapiro, Andrew. "Challenging criminal disenfranchisement under the voting rights act: A new strategy." Yale Law Journal. 103. (1993): 537-566. Print.

45. Fletcher, George. "Disenfranchisement as punishment: Reflection on the racial uses of infamia." UCLA Law Review. 46. (1999): 1895-1908. Print.

46. Behrens, Angela, Christopher Uggen, et al. "Ballot Manipulation and the 'Menace of Negro Domination:

Racial Threat and Felon Disenfranchisement in the United States, 1850-2002." American Journal of Sociology. 109. (2003): 559-605. Print.

47. Nixon v. Condon. Disenfrachisement of the negro in Texas. New Haven: 1932. Print.

Where Did We Go Wrong

COMING SEPTEMBER 2012

You have to know where she came from to figure out why

She is the way she is.

Allisa "Ali" Ibarra is a beautiful, confident and smart girl who lived a troubled life. Remnants of her father's deceit and unforgiveable actions have forced Ali into adulthood much sooner than she anticipated. Ali's life is turned upside down when her aunt Lydia is brutally murdered in the streets of Los Angeles. Lydia became a victim of her own hustle and she learned the hard way that the game she was playing had no winner. In this game the only winner is the game itself! Lydia's death caused Ali's uncle Cortez to become consumed with hate and his desire for revenge became uncontrollable.

Ibarra Ali & Ash is a page-turner that presents the challenges of a dysfunctional family and a little girl who tries to keep her world from falling apart.

Become a fan and learn more about Ibarra at: www.facebook.com/ Ibarra.complete.series

Follow Author DayShawn R. Smith at: www.twitter.com/ Mizuki_Ibarra

WE NEED CHANGE

WOODWARD AV

SOUTH

NOR

WHERE DID WE GO WRON

Charles Bell's novel is a thought-provoking literary work tha initiates discussion on the problems that adversely affect the African American community. In light of the low high scho graduation rates for African American men and the absence effective leadership in the African American community, Be novel proposes the question Where Did We Go Wrong? By providing an insightful analysis of the problems many Afric Americans encounter such as high incarceration rates, unemployment, and political absenteeism, Bell encourages h readers to take ACTION! As Bell states, "Change is a choic —and today we must choose a different course because I fear what the future holds for us as a people." Throughout the exploration of research in the specified areas of interest, Bell adequately conveys the urgency of this situation and the nee for unity in the black community; "Brothers and sisters WE can do better!"

http://www.weneedchange.org
facebook.com/weneedchangeorg

ISBN 9780615662077

90000

9 780615 662077

DETHRONING

The
American Medical
System

Taking Personal Responsibility For Your Healthcare

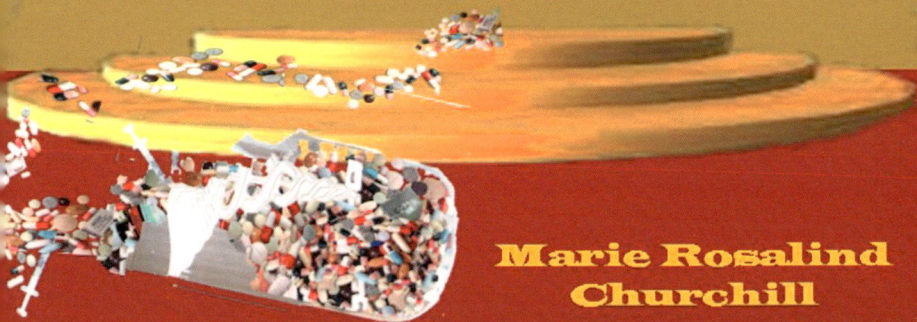

Marie Rosalind
Churchill